MW01408930

A Vibrant Vision
The Entrepreneurship of Multigenerational
Family Business

A Vibrant Vision

The Entrepreneurship of Multigenerational Family Business

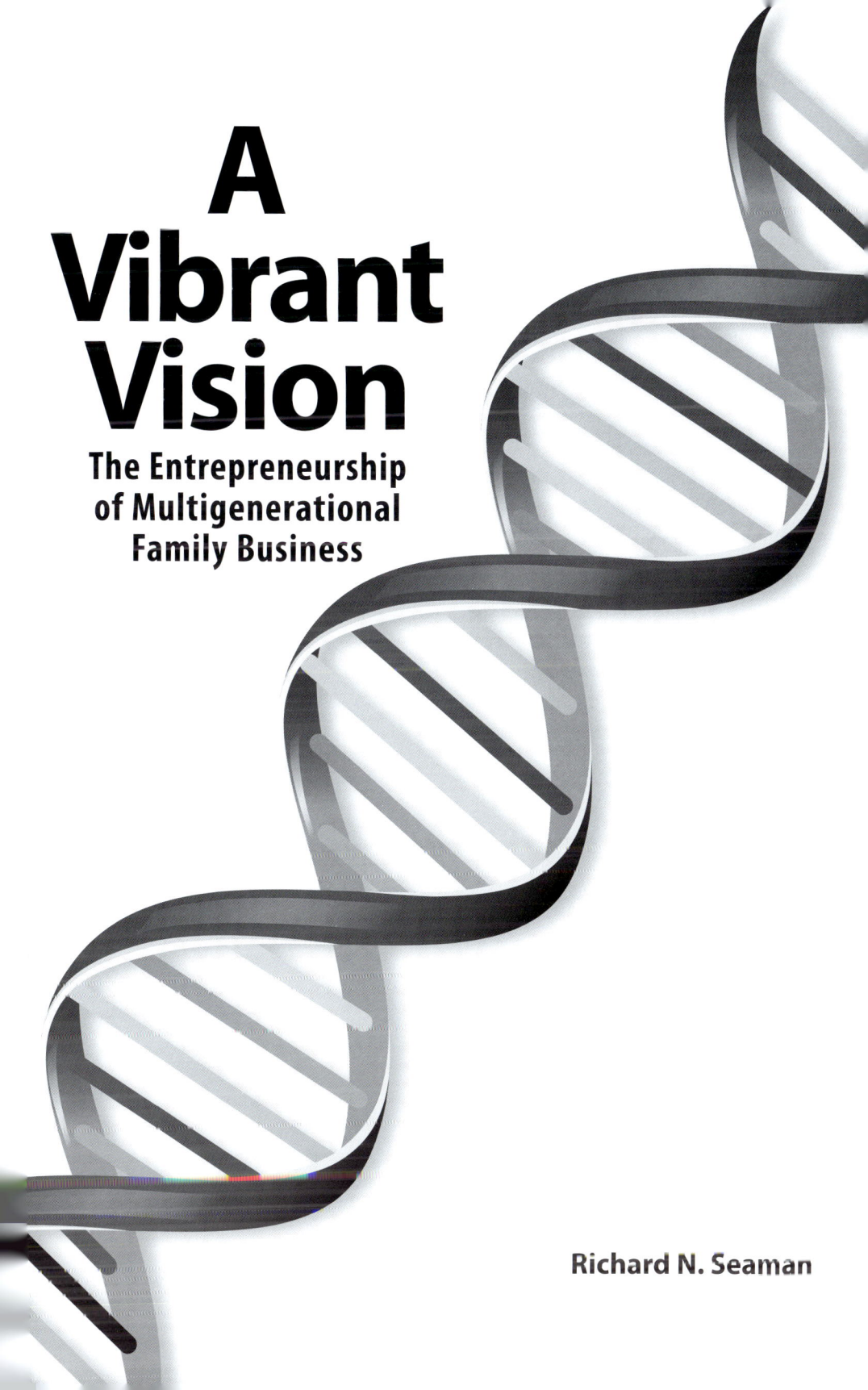

Richard N. Seaman

Published by Seaman Corporation
1000 Venture Boulevard
Wooster, OH 44691
www.seamancorp.com

Copyright ©2019 Richard Seaman

All rights reserved.

No part of this book may be reproduced, stored in a retrieval system, or transmitted by any means, electronic, mechanical, photocopying, recording, or otherwise, without written permission from the publisher.

The FBN logo is a registered trademark of the Family Business Network. The 3M and Parker Hannifin logos are registered trademarks of the 3M Company and Parker Hannifin Corporation, respectively. LeanSigma and the TBM logo design are registered trademarks of TBM Consulting Group, Inc. Quotations from the 2018 EY Global Family Business Survey have been reproduced courtesy of Ernst & Young. The cartoon on page 63 has been reproduced courtesy of CartoonStock, by special permission. The photo on page 93 has been reproduced courtesy of Peter Horree / Alamy Stock Photo, by special permission. All photos are courtesy of Richard Seaman and Seaman Corporation unless otherwise noted.

Design and composition by Seich Ruffo Graphic Design

Cataloging-in-Publication data

ISBN-13: 978-1-7338953-0-9

Printed in the United States of America on acid-free paper

19 20 21 22 23 10 9 8 7 6 5 4 3 2 1

First Edition

To my father, Norman R. Seaman
Whose entrepreneurial spirit not only gave him the courage
to start a family business but whose creative curiosity
became the foundation for our culture of innovation

To my mother, Irene D. Seaman
Who diligently worked by my father's side as a business partner
while raising five children

To my wife, Judy
Who put the "family" in family business
and who served as the sounding board for my visionary dreams
of growing a business for future generations

To our children, Carrie, Kim, and Jason
Who patiently explored and committed
to the stewardship value of being engaged shareholders
of a multigenerational family business

*To the Associates and Leadership Teams
of Seaman Corporation*
Who actively engaged in creating and implementing
the challenging business processes required to build
and grow a multigenerational enterprise

Vision without action is merely a dream.

Action without vision just passes the time.

Vision with action can change the world.

–Joel A. Barker

CONTENTS

INTRODUCTION
Weaving a Vision into a Tapestry of Heirloom Quality 2

CHAPTER 1: INNOVATION
The Enduring Spirit of Multigenerational Business Growth 18

CHAPTER 2: HUMAN CAPITAL
Investing in Those Who Weave the Tapestry of Heirloom Quality 34

CHAPTER 3: STRATEGIC PLANNING
Designing a Tapestry of Heirloom Quality 52

CHAPTER 4: CUSTOMER-FOCUSED QUALITY
Weaving the Tapestry of Heirloom Quality 68

CHAPTER 5: A STRATEGIC IMPERATIVE
Creating Heirloom Quality through Constant Reinvestment 82

CHAPTER 6: GOVERNANCE:
Curating the Tapestry of Heirloom Quality 94

CHAPTER 7: SHAREHOLDER EDUCATION AND ENGAGEMENT:
Stewarding the Tapestry through Generations 112

CHAPTER 8: SUSTAINING YOURSELF THROUGH THE JOURNEY
Nourishing Your Enduring Spirit 134

CONCLUSION
A Lasting Legacy 152

ACKNOWLEDGMENT AND APPRECIATION 160

APPENDIX A
Seaman Corporation Corporate Philosophy 163

APPENDIX B
Governance and Leadership Structure 166

APPENDIX C
*Care Quality Commitment (CQC) Our Never-Ending Quest for
World-Class Excellence* 177

ENDNOTES 182

RECOMMENDED READING 186

ABOUT THE AUTHOR 187

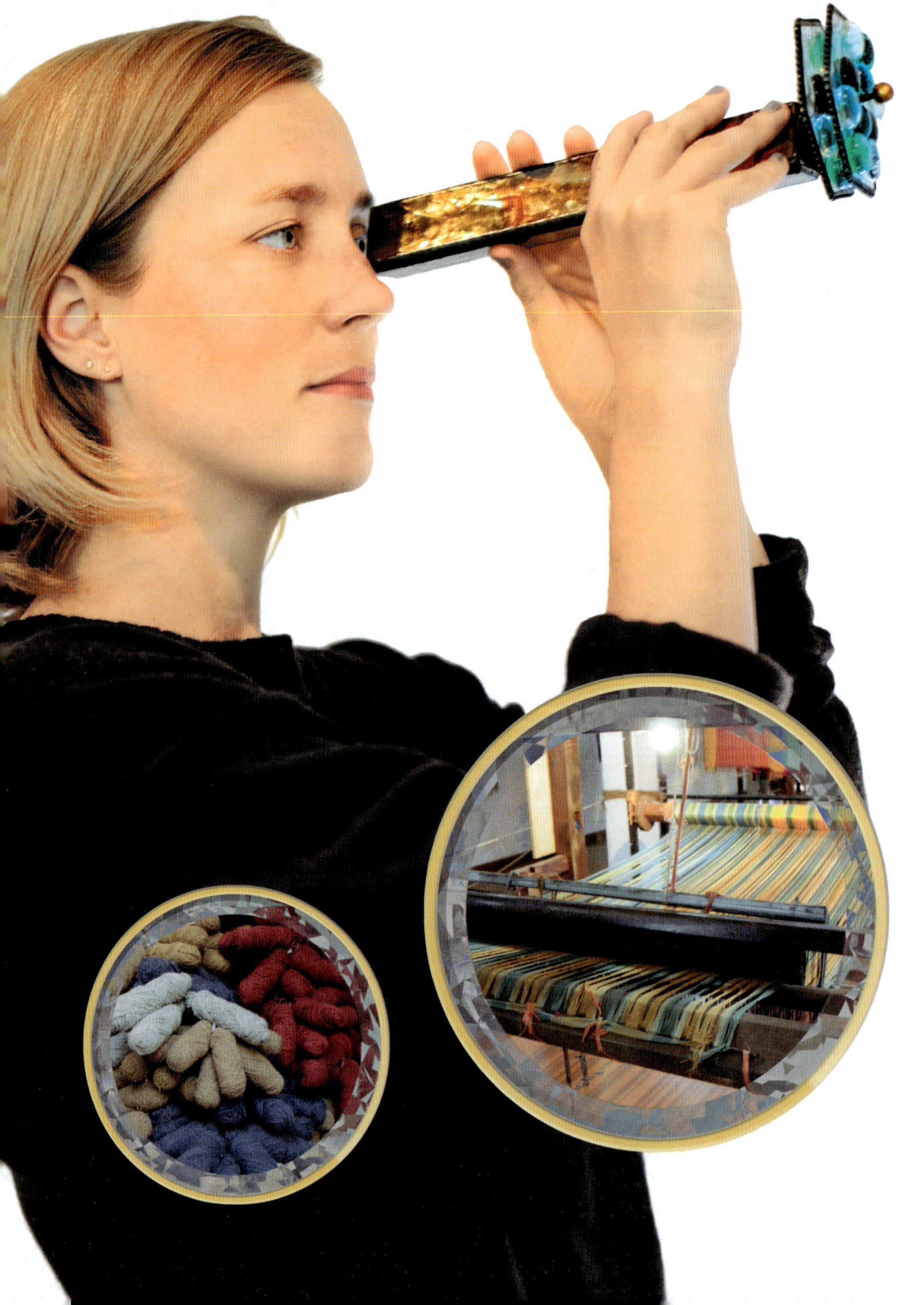

INTRODUCTION

Weaving a Vision into a Tapestry of Heirloom Quality

In the early stages of their business's development, entrepreneurs face a kaleidoscope of choices. Their product or service idea can take on a variety of forms. Their organizational structure is uncertain as they try to look into the future. They see a multitude of colorful patterns that seem to change with every rotational twist.

How can the entrepreneur select from all these "kaleidoscopic patterns" a design that can be woven into a meaningful tapestry that achieves lasting business success? More importantly, how does this creative design become a tapestry of heirloom quality that can continue to expand, evolve, and be sustainable throughout future generations?

Likewise during these early stages, most entrepreneurs are not thinking generationally. They are thinking about the coming weeks, the coming months, the coming year. They are thinking about how to complete the product or service development, how to reach customers, how to acquire funding, how to generate cash flow, and oftentimes how to achieve an exit.

The typical model presented to entrepreneurs as they visualize the path forward for their start-ups is funding from family and friends, seed funding from angel investors, surviving the so-called Valley of Death, followed by institutional funding from venture capitalists (an "A" round), growth, funding from private equity, and, ultimately, the exit: a liquidity event.

Lifecycle of a New Venture

Firm Formation							
Research Grants	Development Grants (eg SBIR)	Friends, Family, & Founders ($5-$50k)	Angel Investors ($50-$500k)	Early Stage Venture Capital ($500k-$2M+)	Venture Capital ($2M-$50M)	Private Equity, Project Financing ($2M-$50M)	IPO, Merger, or Acquisition ($25M+)

← "Valley of Death" →

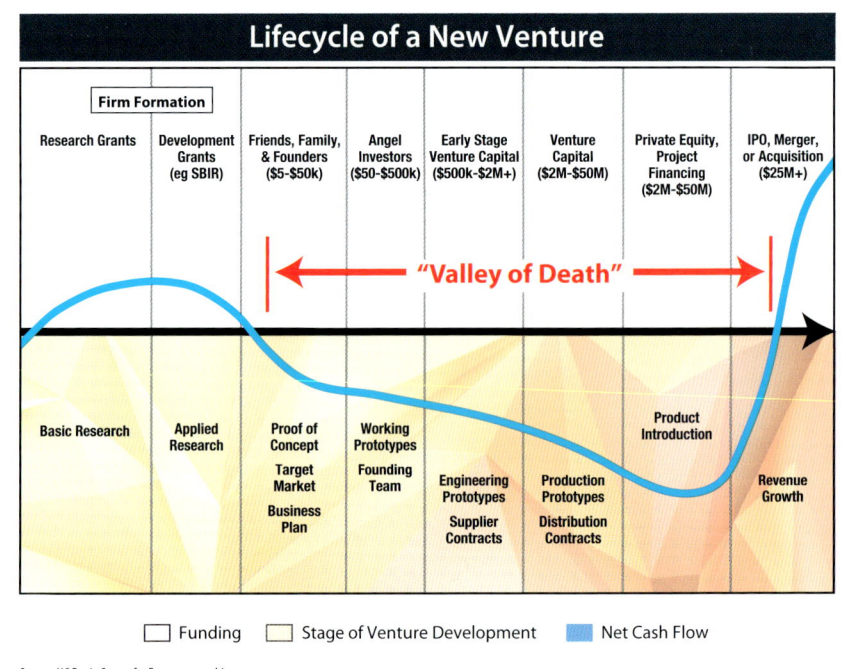

| Basic Research | Applied Research | Proof of Concept / Target Market / Business Plan | Working Prototypes / Founding Team | Engineering Prototypes / Supplier Contracts | Production Prototypes / Distribution Contracts | Product Introduction | Revenue Growth |

☐ Funding ☐ Stage of Venture Development ▬ Net Cash Flow

Source: UC Davis Center for Entrepreneurship

This exit comes in many forms: an IPO, a strategic acquisition by an industry leader, or a sale to another private equity firm.

But all these models of entrepreneurship are focused on a monetizing scenario because these early funders are primarily motivated by financial returns in a five- to seven-year time frame. Little thought is given to creating a stewardship model with an enduring culture or multigenerational heritage.

But the seeds for building an enduring culture or multigenerational heritage are sown in the early years of the business, identifying and creating its own unique DNA. The decisions that entrepreneurs make during these early years, although they feel short term, will be the beginning of a set of business processes woven together to create an organizational future—if only for a few years—until a long-term vision is created.

My mother and father started our business in 1949 with two sewing machines in the basement of our home. Their first contract was sewing lace around baby doll diapers. My father's entrepreneurial vision was simply to acquire enough "cut-and-sew" contracts to generate money to feed his family.

Norman Seaman's First Product: Baby Doll Pants.

My parents' longer-term vision was to build a family business where their five children could build their careers. My mother and father were children of the Great Depression. In their minds, the most valuable legacy parents could leave their children would be a job opportunity that grew into a stable, long-term career.

My father, a high school graduate and a World War II B-24 pilot, had a very curious and innovative mind. His creative thinking was always exploring a kaleidoscope of design choices, experimenting with new and unique products. This curiosity, innovative thinking, and persistence wove a variety of choices together, ultimately creating one of the leading industrial fabrics businesses in North America. His "lace around baby doll diapers" evolved into colorful vinyl-coated industrial fabrics used for a variety of heavy-duty applications such as truck tarps, architectural and environmental fabrics, single-ply membrane roofing, and fabrics for military applications. Today, that company, Seaman Corporation, is a US-based manufacturing business successfully exporting industrial fabrics into China.

RICHARD N. SEAMAN

Upper left: Three air supported tennis court structures in Beijing, China. Upper right: FiberTite roof with simulated metal ribbing. Middle: Shelter-Rite fabric tarp. Lower left: Clearspan fabric structure. Lower right: Clearspan fabric structure for warehousing military equipment.

I am the oldest of five children, and we all grew up in the business. We saw the struggles, the successes, the failures, and the cash flow challenges that my mother and father experienced every day. I watched my father mix formulations in my mother's kitchen. Then he put those formulations into our oven to cure the compounds. Afterward he placed the thin layers of cured compounds in the freezer to see if they remained flexible at cold temperatures. Our kitchen became his homegrown chemical compounding laboratory.

With five children to feed and a struggling start-up business, my parents also farmed our forty-acre homesite. My two brothers and two sisters and I learned a great deal about planting and harvesting vegetables each year as well as raising pigs and chickens for the freezer to feed the family year-round. Our annual chores helped develop our family's work ethic and made us mindful of the sacrifices and work it takes to be committed to a fledgling business endeavor.

Very little strategic planning was done in support of my father's business, certainly no strategic planning around multigenerational success for this business. Nonetheless, my parents did have a vision: Their children would have a business where they could develop their careers. Implicit in this vision were multigenerational hopes and aspirations—for the children of parents who grew up during the Depression and witnessed the challenges of job scarcity and unemployment.

When I turned fifteen, my summer work experience was to assist on the primitive coating lines to help produce the products that provided cash flow to the business and our family. Each summer thereafter was spent in the factory until I went off to college; my summer employment then moved into the office—generally the accounting department. So, I shared real-world work experience with my college education—instilling the principles of entrepreneurship into my academic learning.

It was the summer of 1966. I was between my junior and senior years at Bowling Green State University. I convinced my father to allow me to go on a three-week college trip that would begin in Copenhagen, Denmark; take us to Helsinki, Finland; Leningrad and Moscow in Russia; Bucharest, Romania; Prague, Czechoslovakia; and then finish in Rome, Italy.

The author's 1966 summer trip through Europe and Russia.

I was an excited, young, and naive student who grew up in a village of four hundred in the middle of Amish country. I spent three years at a state college in northwestern Ohio. I was convinced that the Europeans we would meet on this trip would certainly envy us as Americans with all the opportunities that America had to offer.

That illusion was quickly dispelled.

Our first evening in Copenhagen, following dinner, four of us wandered through Tivoli Gardens—the city's Central Park. We were fortunate to meet several Danish students and began talking with them. When we told them we were from America, I was surprised at their response.

"Well, how nice, but we certainly would not want to be Americans."

"Why not?"

"You have many benefits in your country and you're doing quite well, but you are *only* 250 years old. You have no history, no long-term culture."

I was shocked. I had assumed that pride in your country, even at our young age, was measured by financial or material success, or financial opportunity. Here was someone telling me the exact opposite. What she valued as a Dane was the multigenerational, centuries-old history and culture of the homeland. GDP per capita was not part of that consideration. At the time, I did not realize that this multi-generational cultural identity could also apply to the growth and development of a family business. Financial results would not be the singular measure of business success.

Over the years, I came to recognize that these divergent cultures were evident in our paradigms about family businesses in the United States. The success of a family business is measured by its profitability and ability to sustain an ever-growing lifestyle. The motivation to pass it on to the next generation is dependent on one or more of the children willing to have their careers in the business—oftentimes primarily to support the lifestyle of the next generation. If there is no one in the next generation who wants to work in the business, then the obvious exit strategy is to harvest it and pocket the money.

The experience I gained from developing and growing our family business helped me discover other entrepreneurship business models that support multigenerational sustainability by stewarding the culture and heritage of the family business in addition to remaining focused on financial results. This journey is the essence of *A Vibrant Vision*.

After becoming President of my family's industrial fabric business, I had another significant experience that reinforced the insight from my college European trip. As a member of the Young Presidents Organization, I committed to attending the one-week program sponsored at the Harvard Business School each year. I referred to this as "YPO Boot Camp" because of the vast amount of preparation work required before attending—at least forty hours of study for twelve to fifteen case studies prior to arriving. Each year the class consisted of 150 CEOs from around the world. We were divided into study groups of eight, living together and meeting nightly to review cases in preparation for the next day of classes.

This particular year the theme of our program was about when and how to "harvest your business." We were assigned several cases about entrepreneurs who had successfully sold their businesses for millions of dollars. We also studied cases about entrepreneurs who waited too long and missed the window of opportunity for an optimal exit.

In my particular study group, there was a President of a major construction company from South Korea. This President had been educated at Miami University in Ohio. After receiving his degree, he spurned the opportunity to return home to work in the family business and instead took a job in Kuwait, as he had no intention of ever working for the family business. Once he had a son of his own, however, his perspective changed. He decided to return to South Korea and join the family business to continue his family's legacy.

During our study session on Wednesday evening, midway through the week's program, this South Korean classmate interrupted our conversation. He spoke up with a quizzical look on his face. "When I decided to return to the family business, my goal was to manage the business in a manner that will leave it in better condition for the next generation of family members than it was in when I took over. I do not understand this concept of 'harvesting your business.'"

We were all struck by our Korean classmate's perspective. The concept of building a high-growth business only to sell it was totally foreign to him. His words have remained chiseled in my mind. I reflect on them often, particularly as I see the churning of businesses in the United States. Private equity companies buy family businesses, keep them for five to seven years, and then sell them to another private equity company, with little or no appreciation for the culture and heritage of the family business. Many times these businesses become laden with debt until they sink under the weight of their financial burdens, adversely impacting employees and the communities in which the businesses reside.

For example, Hinckley Yacht Company, a boatbuilding business founded in 1928 by the Hinckley family, had a strong brand name and a loyal following. Then, beginning in 1997, the company was sold not once but several times to succeeding private equity companies. According to the *New York Times*, with each sale, the company became more leveraged with debt to support the new purchase price and to fund a rapid expansion.[1] Then when a slowdown in the economy adversely affected the luxury boat market, the company was forced to take drastic measures to service the debt. It sold all its real estate and began moving aggressively against longtime customers to collect marginally overdue receivables, including putting liens on their Hinckley yachts.

The client base reacted negatively and sales fell drastically. The private equity company insisted on major layoffs, reducing the workforce in the small community of Southwest Harbor, Maine, from 625 to 305. The Hinckley family was dismayed by the fate of their once healthy company.

I spend a great deal of time observing start-up organizations, particularly in my work as a trustee of the Burton D. Morgan Foundation and as a commissioner for the State of Ohio's Third Frontier program. I see young entrepreneurs starting new businesses with great creative ideas, many of them software related.

In the vast majority of cases, their vision is to create a software service or a product that can gain marketing traction over the next five to seven years and then have a liquidity event that will make them a multimillionaire. There is virtually no conversation about *creating a business that will grow and be sustainable for generations to come.*

Perhaps this is because so many start-ups require, as discussed, angel financing, then early stage capital, followed by several rounds of venture capital. These sources of funding are looking for a liquidity event that will provide a positive financial return in a short time, certainly less than a generation or two. This source of early funding for entrepreneurial start-ups focuses primarily on five- to seven-year returns. The pressure to create financial value overrides the consideration of longer-term legacy value such as support for the culture of the family business.

Additionally, the United States has a dynamic and responsive market economy, particularly in the financial sector. As reported in *Forbes Online*, in 2017, private equity funds raised $621 billion in this country alone.[2] The large presence and efficiency of private equity makes it much easier to monetize the value/equity of a business and therefore more tempting for a family owner to prioritize a liquidity exit strategy.

A Vibrant Vision advocates for another choice: From the very beginning, consider creating your business with a multigenerational lifespan, built on a solid foundation of family culture and financially sustainable over many generations. I have seen the positive rewards of this choice in our own business and in other family businesses across the world.

In the work my family has done researching family businesses in support of our own, we discovered an international family business organization called the Family Business Network. Although the thirty-year-old organization is based in Switzerland, it sponsors an FBN Summit every year somewhere in the world for its 10,000-plus members. In its thirty-year history, only one summit has been held in North America.

My family had the opportunity to attend the FBN Summit in 2010, held in Chicago, and my wife, Judy, and I attended FBN's International Business Summit in London two years later.

The London FBN Summit was in 2012, when Europe was still reeling from the 2008 financial crisis. The continent was in financial disarray, with everyone very concerned about the Euro and the sustainability of the European Union. But at this international summit, no sessions focused on the financial crisis or the viability of the EU.

I realized that these centuries-old multigenerational businesses had survived many crises in the past: two world wars and a global economic depression in the last century alone. To them, the 2008 financial crisis was simply a speed bump in the road. The businesses recognized the critical nature of the financial challenges and were prepared to respond, but there was very little concern about survival. Sustainability of their family businesses would be dependent on more relevant strategic issues that were the focus of the summit. Unlike the many YPO programs and universities I had been to, the words "harvesting your business" were never uttered.

We had another experience at the London FBN Summit that opened our eyes to the value other cultures place on family businesses. One night, upon arriving at a cocktail reception, I met a young woman who introduced herself as Cleopatra. She was a descendant of a family whose company was three hundred years old. The company had begun as a blacksmith shop that then became the largest iron forger in England. To diversify their family holdings, the family recently had invested in shopping malls in South Africa.

Cleopatra went to college to become a veterinarian. She spent several years following her graduation building a successful veterinary practice. But when her father asked her to join the family business, she did not hesitate to leave her practice and become part of the management leadership. The cultural value of the family business legacy is illustrated by this young daughter's willingness to give up her early career aspirations to continue the stewardship of her three-hundred-year-old family enterprise.

These experiences throughout my career have sustained my early intuitive vision that, like my parents, I wanted to build *a family business that would survive me*. While this vision was not specifically articulated as building a multigenerational family business, the decisions I would make to build "a business that would survive me" implicitly supported a multigenerational family business strategy.

While my vision of building a multigenerational family business seems unique in America's start-up and venture-capital-intensive business culture, according to the *McKinsey Quarterly*, family businesses themselves are very prevalent and economically impactful in the United States.[3] Defined simply, a family business is one wherein the "family owns a significant share and can influence important decisions."

The EY Growth Barometer 2017 (Ernst & Young) explicitly describes the importance of family businesses to our global economy: "Family businesses form the backbone of the global economy; they include some of the earliest, oldest, and largest companies in the world. An estimated two in three companies globally are family-owned and together they are responsible for creating upwards of 70% of global gross domestic product (GDP), according to the Family Firm Institute."[4]

Furthermore, as revealed in the *Family Business Review*, businesses account for eight to nine out of ten business enterprises in North America and generate 64 percent of the United States' GDP, roughly $5,907 billion.[5] While we might think of family businesses as small mom-and-pop shops, some of the largest businesses in America are family owned or controlled: Wal-Mart, Cargill, Ford Motor Company, Comcast, Mars, Milliken & Company, Levi Strauss, and the J.M. Smucker Company among them. In addition, Edelman research has shown that 75 percent of people would prefer to do business with and 54 percent of people would prefer to work for family businesses. In addition, 66 percent of people are willing to pay more for products or services that come from a family business.[6]

Family Business vs. Business in General

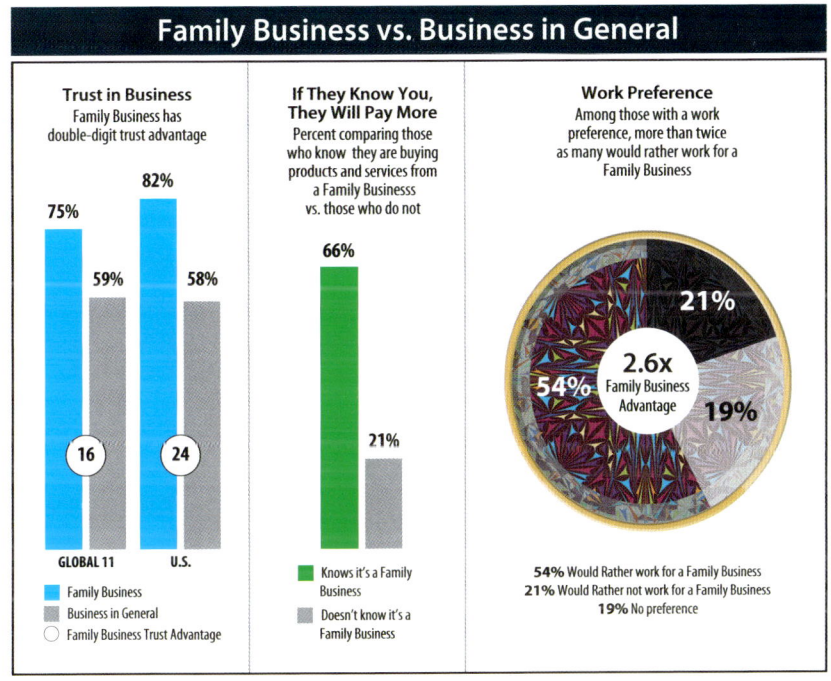

Trust in Business
Family Business has double-digit trust advantage

- Family Business: Global 11: 75%, U.S.: 82%
- Business in General: Global 11: 59%, U.S.: 58%
- Family Business Trust Advantage: 16 / 24

If They Know You, They Will Pay More
Percent comparing those who know they are buying products and services from a Family Business vs. those who do not

- Knows it's a Family Business: 66%
- Doesn't know it's a Family Business: 21%

Work Preference
Among those with a work preference, more than twice as many would rather work for a Family Business

2.6x Family Business Advantage
- 54% Would Rather work for a Family Business
- 21% Would Rather not work for a Family Business
- 19% No preference

Source: 2017 Edelman Trust Barometer Q11-620. 2017 Edelman Trust Barometer Family Business Supplement Q37. On Line Survey in 12 Countries.

If *family businesses* are the backbone of our economy and the preferred partners of consumers, why aren't we more culturally invested in preserving these treasures? Outside the United States, family businesses are preserved through generations. As pointed out in *Family Business* magazine, companies like Japan's Hoshi Ryokan, a 100-room hotel in Komatsu founded in 718 A.D., or France's Taittinger Champagne, founded in 1734, are considered treasures.[7]

Additionally, the American economy was built on such family businesses as John D. Rockefeller's Standard Oil, J.P. Morgan's banking business, and Cornelius Vanderbilt's railroads and shipping businesses. Our own history proves that a family business can be as high-growth as a nonfamily business, with the added benefits of greater stability and an ability to take a longer view on investment decisions.

I know this personally because, as I reflect on my fifty-year career in growing our family business from $2 million in annual sales to nearly 200 million, and employing 350 associates, I have learned a number of lessons about how to grow a business sustainably. I have also concluded that an entrepreneur and business owner must from the outset make a decision about the long-term vision for the business, because strategic decisions for the business will vary depending on that long-term vision.

If your growth vision for the business is to support an ever-growing personal lifestyle for you and your family, then the strategic decisions you make will differ, and this book is not for you. If your growth vision is to have a liquidity event to harvest the business, then the strategic decisions you make will differ, and this book is also not for you. If your entrepreneurship funding model is "family and friends, angel investors, venture capital, private equity, and then EXIT," your strategic focus will differ from the lessons presented in this book.

If, on the other hand, you want to build a business that will continue to grow and be sustainable for multiple generations of family ownership; if you want to build an enterprise that continues to reinvent itself to deliver quality products and services in a changing economic environment; and if you want to create a legacy of stewardship for your future family descendants, then *A Vibrant Vision* will describe the strategies and critical business processes that need to be embraced and institutionalized to support future growth and sustainability.

There can be resistance to embracing these business processes from within the business itself. While the early days of a fledgling family business or any start-up are usually dominated by the charismatic founder's vision and energy, maintaining that momentum can be difficult as the business grows. Nevertheless, as one researcher wisely notes to *BCG Online* interviewers, "the best way to sustain the magic is to formalize it."[8]

I look forward to sharing my experiences in identifying, adapting, and developing business processes that helped a family business that was started with two sewing machines in a basement grow and achieve international success as a leading industrial fabric manufacturing business. My hope is that these experiences will provide inspiration and insight for how you might develop your own set of business principles, processes, and strategies for sustainable multi-generational growth in your own family business.

I truly believe that these are the principles and processes that will help entrepreneurs take the kaleidoscope of opportunities that they encounter and help weave them into a tapestry of heirloom quality that can be passed on from generation to generation.

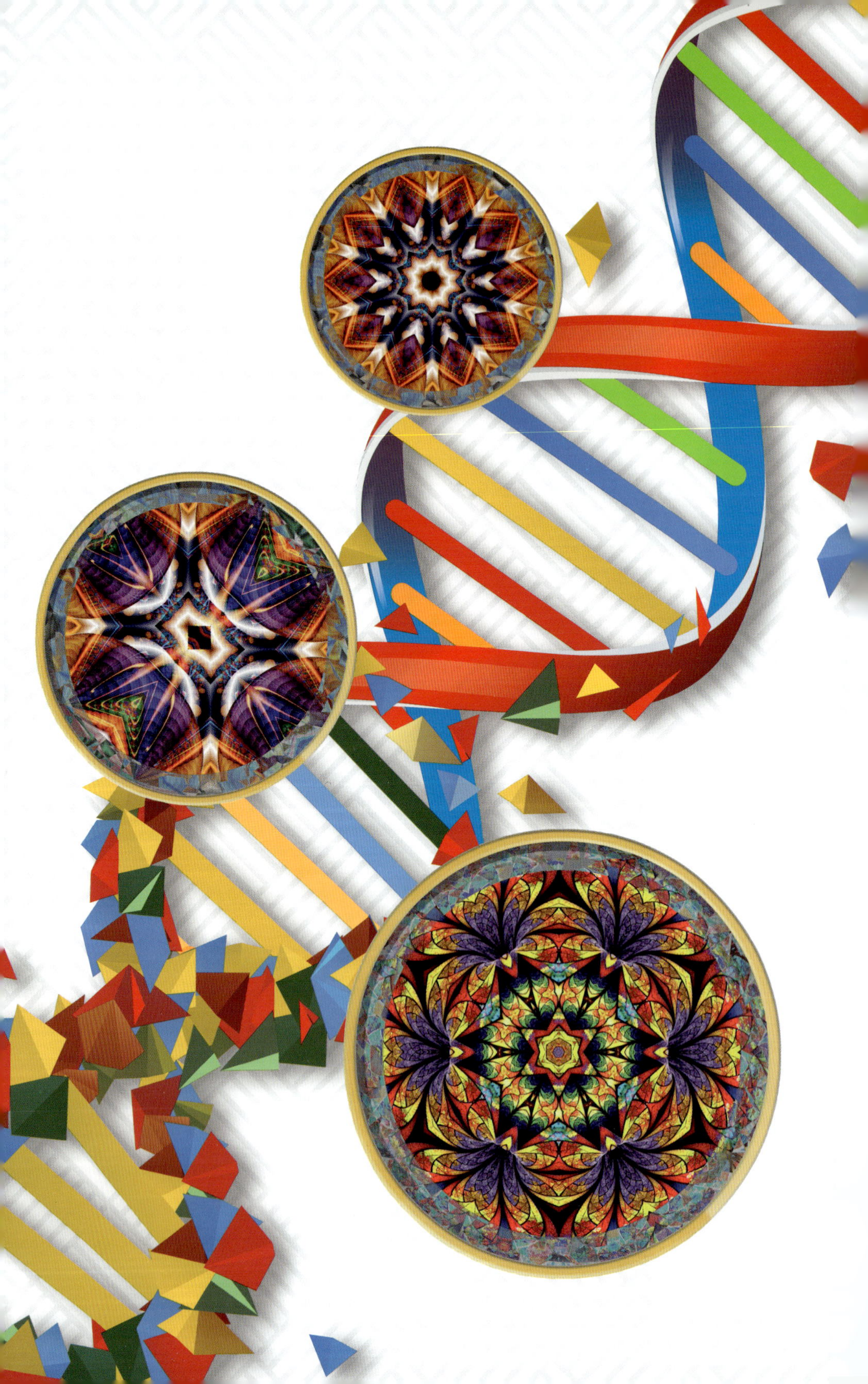

CHAPTER 1

INNOVATION

The Enduring Spirit of Multigenerational Business Growth

Large family businesses create cultures that are agile, foster innovation, and reward fresh thinking. All these conditions fuel disruption in the marketplace . . .

The world's largest, and often longest lasting, family businesses have long learned to adapt and innovate—how else would they still be a force in today's competitive markets? . . . This long-term and entrepreneurial orientation may be intended to create a lasting legacy for the family but also results in creative and prosperous businesses.

—2018 EY Global Family Business Survey

It is commonly believed that family businesses do not survive over several generations. The data confirm this paradigm. According to the 2018 EY Global Family Business Survey, an often-quoted "family business survival ratio" is 30:10:3. That is, approximately 30 percent of all family-owned businesses make it to the second generation; 10 percent are viable into the third generation; and only 3 percent survive into the fourth generation and beyond.

One primary reason family businesses fail to survive into the next generation is the lack of both a good governance process and the appropriate education of future family shareholders. In addition,

I believe a lack of innovation and the desire to continually reinvent the business are also significant causes of failure.

Fortune 500 companies are known for having good governance processes, yet, as American Enterprise Institute scholar Mark Perry notes, 88 percent of those companies that existed in 1955 were gone by 2014.[9] Most of those companies failed to survive two generations. Without a culture of innovation that develops new products and services for our changing global economy, the result will be the eventual demise of any business organization. Therefore, the essence of growth and sustainability over multiple generations requires the commitment to a spirit of innovation.

In today's internationally competitive environment, businesses constantly face new competition and new technologies as well as product and service disruptions. To build a business, to scale a business, to grow and survive into future generations, a business must have a spirit of innovation. To successfully navigate and survive the dynamic challenges in today's world economy, the organization's associates must always be looking for ways to improve products, services, processes, and technologies. This requires a strong cultural component and an institutionalized, company-wide spirit of innovation.

Family Businesses Excel at Innovation

The good news for us is that family businesses are, on average, more innovative than their nonfamily counterparts. A 2017 study published in the *Harvard Business Review* showed that, despite investing less in R&D, family businesses have a higher output of innovation "as measured by number of patents, number of new products, or revenues generated with new products."[10]

Family businesses are viewed unfairly as being "risk adverse, traditional, and stagnant"—as I said, lifestyle businesses—but in fact are able to invest on a longer horizon, more prudently, and with the expertise of generations of industry wisdom. A business that is already thinking about how to preserve itself for generations to come is naturally inclined to monitor disruption. In addition—as Ernst & Young experts propose—family businesses have an "enviable agility to move forward" with investment decisions because of their unique alignment between management and shareholders.[11] Researcher Joseph Astrachan agrees. "They can react quickly as conditions change," he explains, either "seiz[ing] the moment in areas with high potential for growth or mak[ing] long-term potentially disruptive investments."[12]

Successful multigenerational family businesses have shareholders (owners) who have developed the sense of stewardship for the long term rather than the need for short-term financial results. This allows the board and management to make decisions for the long term and creates an environment where innovation can thrive as a result of timely decision making supported by a more patient time horizon.

The result is that many family businesses set the standard for innovation: businesses like Enterprise Rent-A-Car or W.L. Gore and Associates, which manufactures GORE-TEX. Wal-Mart, publicly traded but family owned since its inception in 1945, is an excellent example of this. Wal-Mart's revenues grew from $44 million to $44 billion between 1972 and 1992, in no small part, notes Michael Hammer for *Harvard Business Review*, because of its hyperefficient purchasing and distribution centers.[13] Innovations like "cross-docking" (goods are loaded directly from suppliers' trucks onto Wal-Mart trucks, which deliver them to retail locations without ever being stored) lowered operating costs, which in turn led to Wal-Mart's famously low prices.

A History of Innovation

Seaman Corporation was blessed with a spirit of innovation from its very beginning because of the curiosity of its founder. Norm Seaman was simply a high school graduate with a curious mind and a thirst for product creation. He was always seeking a better product solution that used both current and emerging materials and production processes. He had an intuitive passion for product development.

Remember from the introduction that my dad's entrepreneurship began in 1949 with my parents sewing lace around baby doll diapers on two sewing machines in their basement. This cut-and-sew business was soon fabricating products utilizing the emerging vinyl films. As a result, Norm became intrigued with vinyl chemistry. He experimented with compounding in our kitchen. He cured his compounds in the oven and placed them in the freezer to see if they would perform in cold weather.

Norm soon developed a vinyl-coated nylon fabric that would outperform canvas truck tarps. He built his primitive coating lines from scavenged steel and metal, electric heaters, gas-fired ovens, and drive motors. With this "Rube Goldberg" production equipment he became a primary supplier of this innovative vinyl-coated fabric to major tarp manufacturers around the country.

Once my father completed the development of one product and introduced it into the marketplace, he began looking for other opportunities to utilize coated fabrics. This constant pursuit of innovation led our company to develop unique base cloths for coating, even incorporating knitting equipment to impart special performance characteristics such as improved tear-strength and dimensional stability. He created a unique hot-melt coating technology that was the first in the country to produce coated industrial fabrics. Norm's insatiable spirit of innovation that continually sought out a kaleidoscope of colorful and intriguing opportunities led to the creation of high-performance coated fabrics for architectural structures, for military applications, for marine and environmental applications, and for roofing systems.

When customers experienced challenges in fabricating our materials, Norm would develop the equipment to make their fabrication processes more cost-effective and then sell them the equipment. It is that spirit that is a significant part of the DNA embedded today in our multigenerational business.

Institutionalizing Innovation

By its very nature, early-stage entrepreneurship is the essence of innovation. The entrepreneur has a new idea for a product or service that will bring a value to the market. This entrepreneur optimistically sees a broad range of choices that will determine how the company will produce a product, how it will develop a service, and how it will go to market. Together, the entrepreneur and the company will choose processes for creating and producing their product or service. If this kaleidoscope of choices they select is going to be woven into an enduring tapestry, this spirit of innovation must be a significant part of its DNA and continue to permeate the culture of the company.

Strategic Planning Uncovers Opportunities

Growth and sustainability of a multigenerational organization require an effective strategic planning process. A driving focus of this process must be innovation and new business development. This key result area helps to identify market opportunities and focuses the entire organization on accomplishing product development and market success.

As an example, Seaman Corporation began strategic planning several decades ago. In our first session, the R&D manager presented a new business opportunity for aboveground fuel storage tanks. This application required an entirely different product using materials with which we had little experience. Nevertheless, it could be produced on one of our coating technology platforms.

By discussing this innovative product and the new business opportunity at a strategic planning session, we focused the entire organization on this product development and business development challenge. We were successful in this effort and the product has been responsible for tens of millions of dollars of sales volume over the past three decades.

Flexible Fuel Storage Tank

Strategic planning is the framework that allows the company to communicate and unearth new ideas, but how is this culture of innovation sustained as a business continues to grow and as the organic sharing of new ideas becomes more complex? Many barriers impact the robustness of the innovation process. One of these is the success of the business itself.

In a successful business enterprise, it does not take long for the focus of an organization to shift from innovating to supporting the customer base that is driving the growth. Even if there is a continuing investment in research and development resources, oftentimes those functions become dedicated to the existing customer needs, resulting in the tweaking of products or services in the existing portfolio. While this customer support is very important, it does not truly develop new products and services for the marketplace or for new markets. The true spirit of innovation, as institutionalized, evolves to a customer technical support function.

An organization may feel that its continued investment in research and development is supporting an innovation culture. However, that research and development may simply be supporting the *existing* successful business. Its focus on current customers' needs or improving the efficiencies of existing technology may be creating minor extensions and/or product variations that are replacing the existing portfolio of products and not contributing to sustainable organic growth.

A successful company can become the victim of what Harvard Business School's Clayton Christensen describes in his book *The Innovator's Dilemma*.[14] A company's development resources are consumed with improving existing technologies or products/services for existing customers. In the meantime, subtle changes are occurring in the marketplace and disruptive technologies emerge to meet these market needs more effectively and efficiently. Digital photography and ride-sharing services are but two obvious examples.

If a company's spirit for innovation is to remain robust, it needs to change as the business becomes more successful. A $5-million business that wants its innovation process to contribute 10 percent to the annual growth rate needs to generate $500,000 of new sales. A $50-million business with the same objective will require an innovation process that will generate $5 million annually in new sales. At $100 million in size, that will be $10 million of new products and services. The innovation and new business development processes will need to adjust and become more robust.

Utilize Benchmarking to Find Your "Secret Sauce"

Seaman Corporation was very successful at growing its business to $50 million in size over several decades by applying the innovation process that was a legacy of its founder. This process focused on customer and market needs. It invested both in research and development and in process technology to create new and unique products for the marketplace, like the aboveground storage tanks I mentioned earlier.

One of the current strategic objectives of Seaman Corporation is to have 20 percent of its sales come from products that did not exist five years ago. We developed this metric by benchmarking Rubbermaid when it was among the country's most admired companies. At that time, it mandated that 30 percent of its revenue every year must come from new products. We slightly lowered this metric, as Rubbermaid was consumer-product oriented and its products had a shorter life cycle than Seaman Corporation's. For us, this metric kept the organization focused on new product development. This innovation process successfully supported our company's growth journey.

When the company achieved $100 million in annual sales, it became apparent that the legacy innovation process for new business development would not continue to provide sustainable growth. Even though the strategic metric of 20 percent of sales coming from products that did not exist five years ago was being met, many of these "new products" were replacement products that did not contribute to overall sales growth.

Initiating change in the legacy innovation and new business development processes is a unique business challenge. Like any change initiative, benchmarking "best in class" companies is an important contributor to success. For example, if a company wants to initiate Lean Sigma in its organization, many companies that have successfully accomplished this process-improvement initiative are willing to share their success.

With innovation, however, it is far more difficult to utilize benchmarking. With innovation, no two companies use the same process—there is no "cookie cutter" approach. Every successful innovative company seems to have developed its own "secret sauce" that sustains its spirit of innovation.

For example, I was fortunate enough to visit Milliken & Company as part of our benchmarking process. Plastered all over its walls are quotes by its founder, Roger Milliken, that are important to the company.

> *Technology creates the opportunity, innovators make it happen.*
> *We're not here to massage history, we're here to make history.*

I realized that these quotes were articulating the secret sauce of the company. Great care had been put into selecting and displaying what made this particular company unique in its pursuit of innovation.

Benchmarking is nonetheless critical to achieving a more robust innovation and new business development process. It is important to try to understand what works well in successful innovative companies. But these are not "drop in" solutions. Each organization must evaluate the aspects of successful innovation processes and then determine which attributes can be applied in its own organization that will enhance its unique secret sauce and enhance innovation and new business development.

For example, Apple, Intel, Milliken, and 3M are all considered highly innovative companies. The innovation processes that drive their consistent growth, however, are unique to each company and have successfully evolved within their own organizations over time. As an example, 3M focuses its development on finding ways to create new and innovative products from its existing technology platforms. The "Post-it Note" product line evolved from a chemist attempting to develop a new very strong adhesive. Instead, he discovered a weak low-tack adhesive that could be reused. This product did not find a home until several years later when a fellow chemist used the adhesive to create bookmarks for his church choir hymnal.

An Evolving Innovation Process

Seaman Corporation has a history of successfully adopting change initiatives to support its growth. Among these initiatives are strategic planning, quality improvement processes, and Lean Sigma. But, we have spent the past two decades attempting to make its innovation and new business development processes more robust.

A eureka moment came when we recognized that the organization was still relying on the R&D function to drive our new business development process. While this group continued to do a good job of developing new products and supporting existing customer and market needs, it was not connected well enough to new market opportunities to complete the commercialization process. The R&D staff believed that if they developed a new product, someone else in the organization would then be responsible for getting it to market and convincing customers to buy it.

We decided to take a step back and determine how we might preserve the important parts of our legacy innovation process but add or enhance the necessary components to make it a more holistic and effective new business development process.

As part of this quest we initiated a benchmarking process for innovation and new product development. We began with the Parker Hannifin Corporation, a company in Cleveland, Ohio, that was noted for its new product developments. Our objective was to try to understand Parker Hannifin's approach to identifying market opportunities and then using their capabilities to develop products to meet those market needs. Next we visited Milliken & Company, a traditional multigenerational family-owned textile company that became a global leader in innovation. We were then fortunate to have the opportunity to visit the 3M Company in Minneapolis and learn about their innovation and new business development processes.

While each of these visits provided excellent benchmarking information for us, the company that resonated the most with us at Seaman Corporation was 3M. The presentation made by the 3M staff focused on their technology platforms. While 3M has thousands of SKUs, every product can be traced back to one of forty-six technology platforms, similar to the Post-it Notes that evolved from 3M's adhesive technology.

3M shared a story from its early history to help us better understand the use of technology platforms to develop new products. 3M was started in the late 1800s as a company that manufactured sandpaper. One of its early customers was the Ford Motor Company, to whom 3M supplied the sandpaper for sanding the metal on the cars just prior to painting.

During a visit by one of the 3M engineers, Ford expressed the desire to paint their cars two-tone instead of all black. They did not know how to paint two colors on a car, however, and have a distinct line between the paint colors. The 3M engineer wondered why were they asking him since 3M only made sandpaper.

Nevertheless, when the engineer returned to his office, he began thinking: To make sandpaper, we take paper and apply an adhesive. We then add sand. If we left the sand off of the paper and revised the adhesive a bit? Voilà! We now have masking tape.

A uniquely new product derived from an existing technology platform.

A key component to 3M's new business development process is having an organization that thoroughly understands its forty-one basic technology platforms and its willingness to explore their potential cross-market product applications. Exploiting this secret sauce in the best sense of the word has led to the creation of thousands of specialized 3M products.

After this visit to 3M, I began thinking about our own business. I realized that my father's creative thinking began with our technology platforms. Rather than continue to manufacture only those products that were explicitly meant to be produced on the platforms, he was always experimenting with what *else* could be manufactured on the technology platform.

For example, when he was not able to buy the style of woven cloth he needed, he purchased six of his own weaving looms—and created a fabric-formation technology platform. Once he acquired weaving, compounding, and coating technology platforms—primitive as they may have been—he began tinkering with the available materials.

Once he successfully produced quality fabrics for the truck tarp business, he began thinking about how to use these materials and processes to make coated fabrics for air-supported structures or for inflatable boats. In those very early days, our development staff was creating new products for totally distinct markets just by utilizing existing technology platforms.

In recent years, our organization had shifted the focus to identifying new markets that essentially were adjacent to our existing markets to drive new business development. While this has its advantages, we were limiting our true growth potential because we were not thinking about our technology platform capabilities.

For example, in our roofing business, we purchase adhesives from third-party suppliers and then resell them to our roofing contractor customers to use in our fully adhered roofing product line. When I asked why we did not make these adhesives ourselves, I was told, "We are not in the adhesive business." But actually, we compound a number of adhesives that we apply in the coating of all our fabrics. Why not look at this compounding technology platform and develop adhesives for the roofing marketplace? *This* kind of thinking is what has always differentiated us in the past.

Incorporating the capabilities of technology platforms into the creative process of new product and new business development will significantly expand the organization's innovation capacity. It is what allowed us to grow before, and it will continue to fuel our growth in the future.

The Value of Articulating Your Secret Sauce—
Seaman Corporation's DNA

Should an organization use outside resources to assist in developing a robust innovation process? Many outside resources do a good job of teaching the mechanics of product development such as stage gate processes. Few of them, however, will be able to truly understand the secret sauce of your organization that drives your spirit of innovation for sustainable organic growth. That requires a great deal of "soul-searching" by the entire organization.

Our visit to 3M clarified for me one of Seaman Corporation's key advantages—namely, our technology platforms. My challenge was to articulate and communicate this vision to our organization. Working with my management team, we identified five basic technology platforms: fabric formation, compounding, coating, finishing, and fabrication.

I then expressed these technology platforms as a ribbon of DNA, incorporating materials, processes, and intellectual property (i.e., know-how) unique to each platform. I believe every product we manufacture can be uniquely expressed with its own Seaman DNA molecular ribbon.

These DNA ribbon-like molecules become the threads that will create a unique tapestry of enduring quality.

Leadership—Innovation Starts at the Top

The culture of innovation must permeate all aspects of a company, not just the R&D function. Organizations need to constantly improve their processes to remain competitive in a global economy. Adopting process improvement initiatives such as Lean Sigma requires innovative thinking where associates remain open to the change that innovation and process improvement will bring.

A spirit of innovation must translate into organic business growth. It cannot just be an exercise in curiosity. Innovation must be a strategic driver in the business that creates new products and services for the marketplace. There must be strategic measurements to keep the focus on innovation.

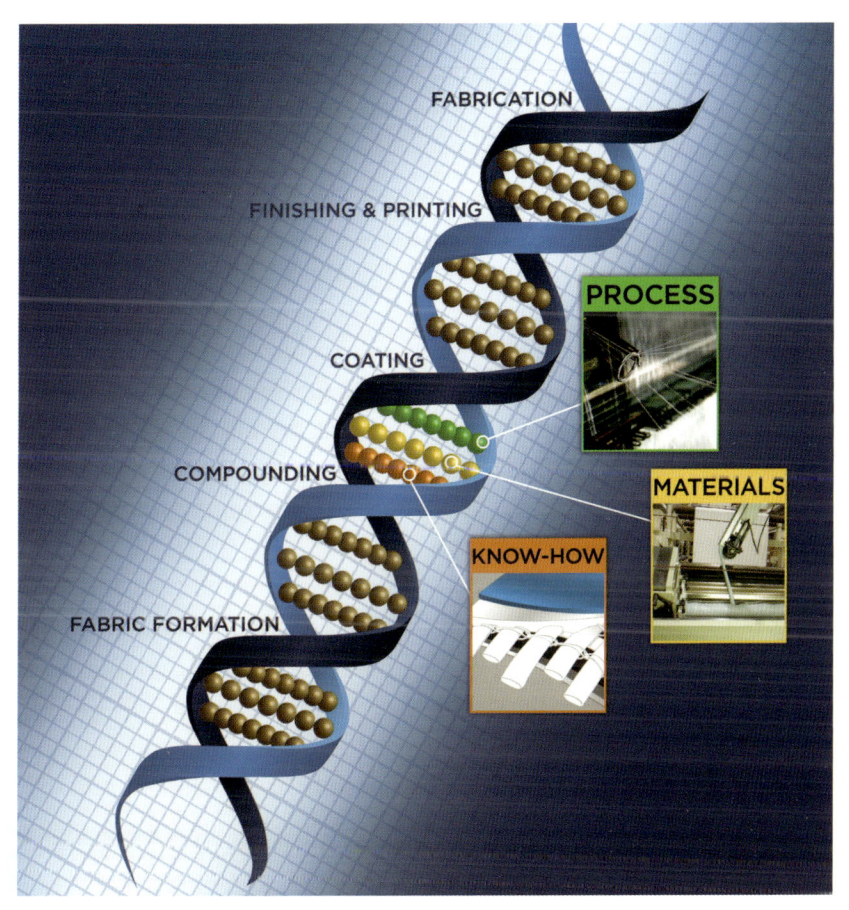

The DNA of Seaman Corporation

A growing successful business experiences a major risk to its innovation culture. Many business functions are required to support a growing business, most of which have immediate day-to-day consequences. If the CEO of the organization delegates the innovation and new business leadership downstream, it will become marginalized to the more pressing day-to-day demands of the business.

If an organization is going to have a robust new business development process driven by a spirit of innovation, *the CEO must be the leader of it*. The CEO must be actively engaged in this new business development process, with a senior leader of that process directly reporting to him or her.

When we were a smaller organization, new business development naturally fell under the direction of the Vice President of Research and Development. As Seaman Corporation continued to benchmark what would drive the evolution of our new business development process, however, we created a new leadership position—a Vice President for Innovation and New Business Development.

The former structure did not provide the leadership and resources necessary for today's business requirements. We need resources in product research but also additional resources for the commercialization process, including the upfront market research on potential market opportunities to identify and confirm potential product and service offerings. The Vice President for Innovation and New Business Development leads both of these functions to drive more effective organic business growth.

Over the last twenty years, our company has had several false starts in trying to create a more robust process of innovation. We did not fully understand the challenge of linking R&D with real market opportunities and the challenges of commercialization—linking the creative work done in R&D to real market opportunities. This requires dedicated individuals who not only have excellent research skills but also are very entrepreneurial, with a strong desire to create new businesses.

Acquisitions as a Growth Strategy

It is not uncommon to think that the best way to grow a business organization is with an acquisitions strategy. But if you have not learned how to grow your own company organically in a sustainable manner, why take on the risks—financial and cultural—that are significant in any acquisition? If you cannot grow your own business, how are you going to grow an acquired business with all its associated complexities and risks? Additionally, in a family business, an acquisition is a risk not only to the business but also to the family assets, an important consideration.

Acquisitions have a variety of risks associated with them—even more so today with the primary competition for acquisitions being private equity firms that have an abundance of capital to leverage and invest. As a result, the competitive price for an acquisition can be six to eight times the EBITDA (earnings before interest, taxes, depreciation, and amortization).

For a private equity purchaser, this requires confidence in a reasonable amount of sales growth in the next five to seven years that will generate significant free cash flow. Eighty to 90 percent of that cash flow will be required to pay down the leveraged debt, with little available to invest in growth strategies and operational improvements that increase productivity. In addition to these financial risks, company culture differences and HR development represent other dimensions of significant risk that can detract a business's leaders from the core business.

For example, as of this writing, Seaman Corporation has made the capital investment to produce $200 million in sales revenue. In 2017 our annual revenue was $150 million and we employed 350 associates. Our strategic objective was to grow to $200 million in the next three to five years. We *could* accomplish that goal quickly with a $50-million acquisition. But a robust and effective innovation and new business development process should be able to accomplish that growth objective without taking on all the risks associated with a large acquisition.

Once our organization is confident in our innovation and new business development process, then an acquisition strategy that focuses on applying this process to acquired companies significantly increases the creation of value in acquired companies.

Businesses constantly face new competition, new technologies, and new disruptive product and service offerings. Innovation is required to sustainably scale a growing business and to assure its survival into future generations. An institutionalized company-wide spirit of innovation is required to successfully navigate and survive the dynamic challenges of today's world economy that every multi-generational business will face.

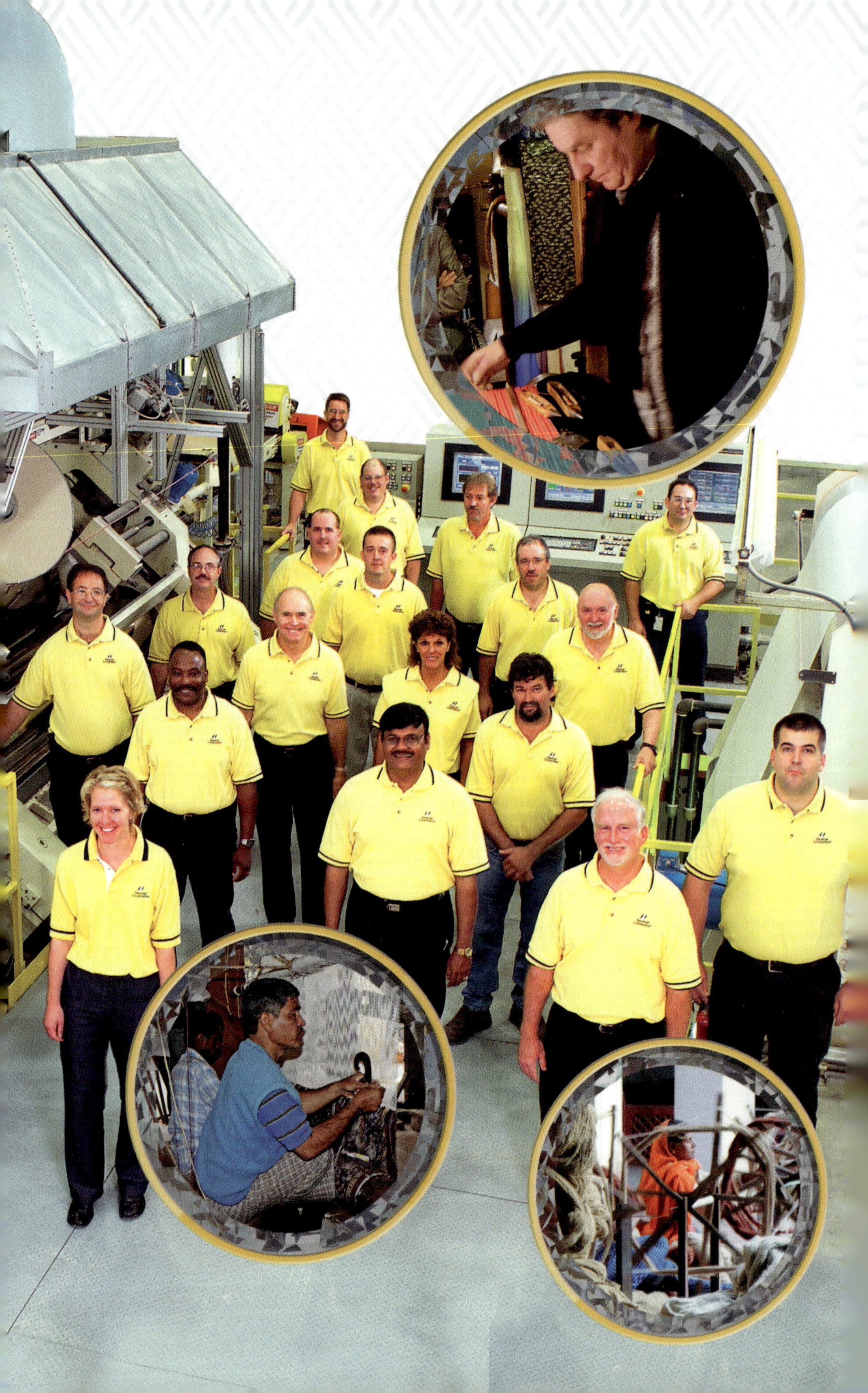

CHAPTER 2

HUMAN CAPITAL

Investing in Those Who Weave the Tapestry of Heirloom Quality

Recognizing the importance of investing in the development of a strong human resource (HR) function is not the primary focus of an entrepreneur starting a business. The focus on personnel may be searching for employees with talent specific to the product or service offering being created. Little thought is given to investing in the *HR processes* that will be required to support the sustainable growth of the business.

My early career experience in our family business is evidence of this entrepreneurial characteristic. Shortly after my father started our business, he hired his father, who had had production management experience during World War II. Because my entrepreneurial father wanted to spend his time on product development, he assigned my grandfather production management responsibilities, which included personnel management.

After my grandfather passed away in the early 1960s, very little attention was paid to this personnel management function. Any labor needs were identified and filled by each supervisor as they arose.

As the business grew, the management responsibilities naturally increased, and they were assigned to existing managers. The availability of quality management talent in a small community with a population of 4,000 was limited, so my father responded opportunistically when talent did surface. He would learn about a local managerial candidate, oftentimes because the candidate had lost his previous job as a result of poor performance (or a drinking issue). Then my father would "rationalize" a new management position for this candidate, a "cost-effective" addition to our management team.

This typical approach led to some memorable humorous personnel experiences. I remember one occasion when my father learned that a senior-level vinyl chemist was looking for work. Despite concerns about his drinking problem, my father hired him because of his resume and very reasonable compensation requirements. His experience would be valuable to a young start-up coating company despite his absentminded nature. I recall sitting in important management meetings and watching this very significant team member doze off.

This chemist supervised our mixing department, mostly populated by hardworking blue-collar workers who had migrated to Ohio from the hills of West Virginia. One day a mixing department employee turned in his handwritten time card indicating that he worked twenty-five hours that day. While this was certainly suspect, it became more fascinating when we learned that his supervisor—our vinyl chemist—had approved the twenty-five-hour workday!

In the absence of a solid HR function, it is common for a young entrepreneurial company to find itself reacting to the management leadership demands. Most often, these leadership demands gravitate to existing management team members regardless of their capabilities or experiences.

An example in my father's case was his very capable secretary. Over the years, many management responsibilities migrated to her desk. Customer service, production management, and even accounting functions became her responsibility. When my father took a two-week vacation, she literally ran the business.

But, this natural migration of leadership to whichever current employee raises his or her hand becomes a strong headwind to the successful growth of the business.

For example, after graduating from college and joining our family business full-time as plant manager, I learned that my father's secretary was managing our accounting department. This made sense in the early days of the company, but now as the business became more complex, we were not receiving reliable financial information until six to seven weeks following the close of a month. This delay made it almost impossible for management to make decisions to improve profitability.

So, I assumed this management role and then created more efficient accounting reporting processes. In a very short time, we had pertinent financial information within two weeks of the close of the month. This timely information facilitated management's ability to make decisions that did improve growth and profitability. It also permitted my father's secretary to focus on those responsibilities she was more capable of managing, such as customer service.

In the ten years I worked with my father, we had two operating plants with more than two hundred employees. Yet, we didn't have any semblance of a personnel department, even to manage the "custodial" responsibilities such as recruiting, payroll, and benefits that were required to support those employees.

In my experience, it is not uncommon in family businesses for this to be the model. As long as the founding patriarch or matriarch runs the business, there can be resistance to professionalizing some of these business functions. I have heard time and again from next-gen family shareholders that no movement will be made toward creating, for example, a strategic HR function until the patriarch can no longer interfere.

Professionalizing the HR Function

My father passed away in 1978. Together we had grown the company from $2 million to $10 million in annual revenue over the course of ten years, and we employed more than two hundred associates at the time of his death. When my father was diagnosed with terminal lung cancer, I was elected President and continued to co-lead the company with my father during his eighteen-month battle.

As I reflected on my first decade at Seaman Corporation, it became clear that our business growth was characterized by a spurt of growth, then a plateau, another spurt of growth, followed by yet another plateau. The limitation always seemed to be our people: growth challenges exceeding the capabilities of our management team—that is, the inability of our management team to lead us to the next level.

If growth is going to be dependent on the quality of our people, then our personnel must be our most important asset. Why, then, did we not have any manager whose primary responsibility was focused on this critical asset? No manager who focused on identifying human capital needs, then interviewing, hiring, and developing our working associates?

So, my first initiative following my father's death was to define and develop an HR function for our business. I quickly started the search for a candidate to fill this management role. I wanted this function to be strategic to our business and not just a "custodial" responsibility. While interviewing, hiring, compensation and benefits management, and compliance are important responsibilities, they alone do not make personnel management strategic.

Rubbermaid was a $300-million public company in our area experiencing rapid growth during this time period. I had begun informally benchmarking them. Their HR function was led by a Vice President of Human Resources who reported directly to the CEO. I became further convinced of the importance of this function to the successful execution of a business strategy. Consequently, I knew there was no other choice but to have the HR function and its leader report directly to the CEO.

Later experiences proved me right. The importance of the HR function would be reaffirmed time and again. In the mid-1980s, we had an aging manufacturing plant in Millersburg, Ohio, and a somewhat newer facility in Bristol, Tennessee. Because there was not enough water to support a sprinkler system in our Ohio plant, our annual insurance premium for that plant went from $20,000 to $120,000 overnight.

We had an option to consolidate our Ohio operation with our recently expanded Tennessee plant, but that would result in the loss of a hundred jobs, including many long-term employees. So I decided instead to make a $4-million investment in a new manufacturing facility in Wooster, Ohio, some twenty miles north, which would preserve nearly all the jobs. At that time, this was the largest single investment ever made by our family business.

After eighteen months of planning, constructing, and installing upgraded equipment, our new manufacturing plant was up and running. I expected a significant improvement in production, in quality, and in employee morale.

Much to my surprise, our production and quality declined. Six months into the transition, my HR manager came to me and said that he had just received a telephone call from the National Labor Relations Board. They wanted to schedule a union election. I was shocked to learn that the NLRB already had the signed election request cards. The union had conducted a successful employee signature campaign and not one of my managers was aware that such a campaign was occurring.

While we subsequently won the organizing election, it became clear to me that simply investing in property, plant, and equipment was not going to assure a successful business. It was equally, if not *more*, important to continually invest in our human resources if we wanted to achieve our goals. This experience led to our discovery, evaluation, and implementation of a quality-initiative process that first and foremost focused on the associates of our organization. (This initiative will be described in more detail in the chapter on "Customer-Focused Quality.")

These early lessons stressed the strategic importance of the HR function. Strategic HR management:

- participates in the strategic planning of a business;
- helps determine the type of organizational structure that will be needed to execute the company's strategy;
- identifies the requirements and human resources needed for this organizational structure;
- develops and executes the hiring strategy; and
- creates the training and development programs necessary.

The leader of the HR function gauges the "pulse" of the organization:

- What is the morale of the organization?
- Do the associates feel valued?
- Are the associates in alignment with their managers and supervisors?
- Does management understand the needs of the associates required to execute the business strategy?

These strategic imperatives must be institutionalized in the businesses to ensure that they are continually monitored. For us, the most efficient way to do this is to integrate the HR function with the strategic planning of the business.

Aligning the HR Function with Strategic Objectives

While it is important for the HR department to be an advocate for the associates, this must be done in alignment with the strategic objectives of the business.

The finest quality product or service offering will not sustainably grow a business without a quality leadership team. Without having the right organization and the right people, the company will fail in its scale-up efforts. So, it is extremely important that the HR function be closely linked with the strategy development process.

The chief human resource officer helps define what it will take to execute the business strategy. A strategic HR function will define today's organizational structure and identify the "people on the bus." Are they the right people and are they in the right seats to execute the strategy?

The HR function can identify the early warning signs and issues that are affecting morale, talent capability, and work capacity. These responsibilities are separate from the more tactical personnel management issues of compliance, compensation, and benefits management. The HR function and its leader must be empowered and engaged in the strategic issues facing the business.

As part of developing an effective and strategic human capital function, the HR process must include detailed information on the employees of the organization. Benchmarking companies like General Electric and Goodyear provides a model of the type of employee database that is needed to support this process.

Utilizing the appropriate software platform, the HR department compiles pertinent information about each employee: education background, years of service, career experience, performance ratings, career growth aspirations, and training and development accomplishments. When the leadership team meets to discuss the personnel needs of the organization, it can make more effective personnel decisions when this database of information is readily accessible.

At Seaman Corporation, the chief human resource officer reports directly to the CEO and is a vital member of the leadership team. The HR function is closely linked to the strategic and business planning processes. Twice a year, the company conducts a Strategic Evaluation of Associates, what we call our "SEA Sessions." This process models the "C" sessions at GE that were developed during Jack Welch's tenure as CEO.

Objectives of Session C Meetings at GE:
- To review the effectiveness of the organization and any plans to change.
- To review and provide feedback on the performance, promotability, and developmental needs of the top management.
- To review plans and suggestions for backup planning for key management jobs.
- Early identification of high-potential talent to ensure appropriate development.
- To focus special attention on key corporate or business messages.

Leadership Development & Succession Planning
Session C Meetings started in April and lasted through May every year. Jack Welch along with 3 senior executives traveled across the US to meet with the top managers of each of GE's 12 businesses and to review their performance over the previous year to identify and promote leadership talent within GE.

Adapted from: https://www.workforce.com/2008/06/12/training-the-top-at-ge/ and www.icmrindia.org/.../Leadership%20and%20Entrepreneurship%20freecasep4.htm]]

The senior leadership team conducts the SEA Sessions confidentially. Each functional leader reviews the associates in his or her department from the readily available database. In addition to presenting the existing staff to the senior leadership team, two potential successors are identified for each position. Preferably, these are internal candidates being trained and developed for future growth. If there is not an internal candidate, the manager tries to identify potential external candidates.

Conducting SEA Sessions in a confidential, cross-departmental manner helps assure that the evaluations will be more objective. Observations and input from peer leaders help identify additional growth and development opportunities for the associates. This process also identifies other potential career paths for the associates.

These SEA Sessions are linked directly to the business planning cycle (as described in the next chapter). At the end of the strategic planning process, a full-day SEA Session is conducted. During this session, the leadership team evaluates the organizational structure. Will the organizational structure support the long-term strategic goals? Then the team evaluates staffing requirements to support the organizational structure. This process provides the leadership team with advanced insight into the future personnel and staffing needs of the organization. Will we have the right people in the right roles at the right time to meet the future needs of the business?

Another SEA Session is conducted during the annual business planning process that develops the budget for the upcoming fiscal year. At this session, firm commitments are made about personnel additions as well as training and development for the coming year.

Conducting the SEA Session twice a year allows the organization to anticipate future growth needs—and plan for them. Integrating the SEA Sessions with the business planning processes assures that the investment in the human capital assets of the company are made in alignment with the business strategies. The HR leadership is responsible for facilitating these highly significant business processes which are required to assure multigenerational growth.

Cultivating Leadership

Even with solid human resource leadership, the CEO must stay actively engaged in the HR function. HR management is a dynamic process, and even more dynamic in a rapidly growing company. There will always be changes in the organization and in the staff, some that occur naturally and some that are required because of changing needs.

The leadership and human resource requirements of a $100-million company differ greatly from those of a $50-million company. If you are not growing your people, you will not grow your company. Managers who do not continue their personal growth will not be capable of meeting the future leadership challenges of a dynamic, growing business.

Training and Development—Executive Coaching

If growing the people of an organization is vital to the sustainable growth of a business, then a significant ongoing investment must be made in training and development. The first response to an underperforming manager should be additional training and development. If performance does not then improve, perhaps the wrong person is in that management role.

A very important component to leadership training and development is coaching. Years ago I attended a conference in San Francisco with more than a hundred CEOs from across the country. This particular afternoon, our resource was David Pottruck, the co-CEO of Charles Schwab, a high-growth retail brokerage firm.

After his presentation, one member asked David: "What do you do to keep your leadership skills strong?"

His response: "I have a leadership coach."

A leadership coach was an uncommon resource back then, so the answer took us all by surprise. He went on to explain how the best golfer in the world (at that time) was Tiger Woods, and Tiger always traveled with a coach. No matter how well Tiger played in a tournament, it was important to have a coach observe his game to keep him from regressing to bad habits or to help him see opportunities for further improvement. Similarly, why should a business leader not have a coach to make leadership observations?

Not only did David Pottruck have his own personal coach, he also provided a leadership coach for all his senior leaders. He permitted each manager to select the coach with whom he or she felt most comfortable. This was something I decided to integrate into my own personal leadership training.

Fortunately, I had a board member who was trained in psychology and organizational development. I engaged him to observe my leadership style in a variety of meetings and associate interactions. His observations provided excellent insights into how I could improve my leadership effectiveness.

Because of the value I personally perceived from this kind of coaching, we began offering leadership coaches to our managers. Initially, we encountered resistance. After all, the idea of being coached was not intuitively understood or embraced by most managers. In fact, the reaction from the first manager to whom we assigned a coach was "there must be something wrong with my performance."

After offering coaching sessions to several managers, however, the management team recognized that a leadership coach was actually an investment in the future growth potential of an associate. Managers soon began requesting a leadership coach. This investment in leadership development has been critical to growing our managers to meet the leadership challenges of our growing business.

Eventually we developed a system wherein the manager was offered three to four different coaching options. Each resource would create a proposal for the manager, and the manager would have the opportunity to interview and select the resource he or she preferred. This was important because the managers needed to be able to build a relationship of trust and confidentiality with their coach.

At the same time, although the personal relationship between the coach and the manager was and is paramount, the coach also has to remember who the client is (the business itself) so that he or she can share details or takeaways as appropriate. Learning to balance this relationship with the demands of the business was something we got better at as an organization as we had more experience with coaching.

The Second-in-Command—Developing the COO Function

Succession planning is one of those leadership challenges for any business. Successful entrepreneurs of a growing business always face the challenge of developing a "second-in-command," or chief operations officer (COO). The challenges of a growing business strain the time and capability of a single individual. Founders of companies will want a competent number two manager for one or more of several reasons:

- They recognize the need for someone to "complement" their own skill set.
- They are "bored" by the necessary administrative requirements of a growing business.
- They want to continue to focus their time on developing new products or services.
- They want more free time to enjoy the fruits of their success.
- They may also be concerned about succession planning.

This last reason is not necessarily a problem you will find in the early stages of the business; rather, it is one you encounter later on when you begin to think about the longevity of the company. Succession planning is a key piece of creating a multigenerational family business.

Once you find yourself at the point of developing a COO, you must ask: Is there a second-in-command candidate within the organization? Will I need to look externally? How will an external candidate be accepted by the organization?

While much has been written about CEO leadership, little has been written about the challenges of second-in-command leadership.

This topic, however, is the research of Dr. Nathan Bennett, Associate Dean for Program Innovation at Georgia State, and Stephen A. Miles, Founder and CEO of The Miles Group, who published their findings in *Riding Shotgun: The Role of the COO*.[15] Through their research, they identified seven archetypical roles for COOs:

> **The Executor:** lead the execution of strategies developed by the top management team
>
> **The Change Agent:** responsible for leading a specific strategic imperative
>
> **The Mentor:** mentor a young or inexperienced CEO (oftentimes the entrepreneurial founder)
>
> **The Other Half:** a leader with skills that complement the CEO's experience, style, knowledge base, or penchants
>
> **The Partner:** a "two in a box" or coleadership model
>
> **The Heir Apparent:** selected to be groomed or tested as the company's CEO-elect
>
> **The MVP:** offered as a promotion to a valuable executive that the company does not want to lose[16]

To develop a successful organizational structure and find the right candidate for the second-in-command, it is important to clarify which of the above purposes is the reason for creating a COO position in your business. This decision will have a very significant impact on the future growth and the sustainability of a multigenerational business. It is one of the most important leadership decisions a CEO and board will make.

The complexity of this decision and the challenges in managing this relationship explain why many entrepreneurs fail in the execution of this important human resource strategy.

I have seen many company owners either promote an internal candidate or recruit an external candidate and announce to the organization that this newly anointed second-in-command is now in charge of the day-to-day operations. The newly anointed also believes he or she has been empowered to lead the organization.

The primary cause of failure in this new organizational relationship is that the *strategic* interaction between the CEO and the COO is episodic and may not occur for months at a time. As the business grows, the alignment between the two begins to diminish.

It may be that the COO is not capable of managing the new growth challenges. But even if the COO is doing a very good job of leading the organization, he or she will likely be making the decisions differently from the way the CEO would. With only episodic interaction at the strategic level, an underlying tension begins to develop between the two. In the end, either the CEO terminates the COO or the COO resigns in frustration. Without a deliberate process that creates the venue for regular strategic interaction, this scenario will be the common result.

In the case of Seaman Corporation, the COO position evolved out of the growth challenges of the business and also the growth desires of an internal candidate. I hired a highly competent individual to fill a vacant comptroller position to lead our finance and accounting department. His business acumen and leadership capability resulted in promotions to Director of Finance and subsequently Vice President of Operations.

Because I knew it was time for our family business to have an empowered and effective second-in-command, I promoted him to COO. But I did not want this new relationship to follow a path of failure. Functionally, he was already fulfilling the role of a COO, but he felt limited by the constraints of his title. In reality, both he and the business were ready for him to assume more responsibility.

Consequently, I created a CEO-COO quarterly retreat process. These retreats were two to three days long and were always off-site. The event included time committed to business issues and also recreational activities. The recreational activities included golf, sailing, fly-fishing, NASCAR driving school, and many others. The time spent away from the workplace, combined with the recreational activities, built a level of understanding, trust, and respect that cannot be developed in the day-to-day office environment.

I was responsible for developing the agenda for the retreats and providing it to the COO in advance. Initially, the agenda included both tactical and strategic issues. We also engaged a facilitator for our first retreat sessions—part of my ongoing commitment to leadership coaching.

The benefits from these regular off-site retreats were many. In the beginning of our working relationship, we found ourselves often disagreeing about tactical or strategic issues. But, over the course of our uninterrupted time together, we learned that these were not so much disagreements as different perspectives on the issue. As we listened carefully we came to respect each other's ideas and most often discovered solutions that were better than either of our individual perspectives.

At the end of each retreat, I had confidence in how my COO was going to run the business over the next ninety days. I also knew we would have the opportunity to evaluate the decisions we made in another ninety days. Equally important, the COO knew he could go forth and lead the organization with my approval and not be concerned that I was looking over his shoulder or second-guessing him.

As time went on and our trust deepened, we were able to focus more on the longer-term strategic challenges facing the business.

The value and significance of developing this special CEO-COO relationship can be summarized in the words of Stephen Miles, co-author of *Riding Shotgun*: "It's no longer accurate to state that CEOs must worry about the future while COOs must worry about the present. Balancing short-term goals with long-term strategy now falls on COOs and entire executive teams. The most successful companies maintain unflinching trust and flawless handoffs between the CEO and COO."[17]

Our CEO-COO retreats accomplished this trust and balance for our company. We never missed a quarterly retreat in the fifteen years of this inaugural CEO-COO relationship, which ended with his retirement. During that time, we successfully quadrupled the size of Seaman Corporation.

Family Businesses and the Commitment to Human Capital

The emphasis in family businesses on long-term growth also influences their hiring and development programs. As you have read, retaining and developing talent has long been a core value of Seaman Corporation, but we are not alone in this. A 2017 study of growth plans for family-owned businesses commissioned by Ernst & Young showed that 72 percent of family businesses were planning to hire staff that year versus 56 percent of nonfamily businesses.[18] Imagine the effect on unemployment rates in the United States if family businesses were given the political and cultural support they merit.

At the same time, many of the family business leaders surveyed were quick to point out that any additional plans they had for increasing automation and operating efficiency were *not* to come at the cost of "replacing our workforce." Success for the company is not just financial but also includes customer satisfaction and a "deep sense of social responsibility" to their community.

Referring again to the *BCG Online* article cited earlier, the relationship between the employee and the employer in a family business is atypical in that it has a high degree of mutual loyalty.[19] An informal "social contract" exists between the two groups, and family employers are more likely to go to extra lengths to care for their employees. The return on this investment is that employees are more likely to continue their career in the family business.

For example, in 2017 our family invested in a six-court indoor tennis facility located right next to our plant property as an asset for both the business and the community. With that in mind we also included a workout gym and offered free membership to our associates. This investment supported the company's wellness program and became a recruiting tool that supported the HR function.

The Aspen Racquet Club indoor tennis facility built in 2018 for the Wooster community and for the Seaman Corporation wellness program.

Family business owners with a vision for a multigenerational legacy must recognize early on that successful future growth will be dependent on the quality of the people who work in the business. Hence, there must be an early investment in a robust human capital function whose leadership reports directly to the CEO.

The HR function actively participates in the strategic planning process. It helps define the organizational structure needed to execute the business strategy. It will develop and execute the talent management plan, which includes developing and executing the recruiting and hiring strategy. The HR function is responsible for designing and implementing training and management development programs.

An effective human capital function constantly measures organizational morale. Are the business associates' work assignments aligned with the business strategies? Do the associates understand the business goals and objectives and does management understand how to help them achieve their role in executing the business tactics? This HR function is also responsible for identifying, training, and developing future generations of management leadership, be that family or nonfamily.

Effective human resource leadership will perpetually prioritize sustaining the culture of a family business as it grows in both scale and geographic locations. HR can accomplish this by continually promoting the history of the company and showcasing examples of stories that reflect the company's philosophy and principles. HR can facilitate celebrations of milestone events. This company lore should also be woven into new associate orientation.

When we renovated our corporate offices, we specifically designed spaces for showcasing our early products. We also have designed graphical displays at each manufacturing facility that pictorially present a historic timeline of the growth and development of Seaman Corporation.

The people of an organization who will be responsible for growing a business are as colorful and diverse as the changing patterns within a kaleidoscope. They are the weavers who will create a colorful tapestry. An effective human capital function, with its variety of facilitated processes, can be seen as the loom that takes the selected vibrant yarns and weaves them into an imaginative tapestry of heirloom quality.

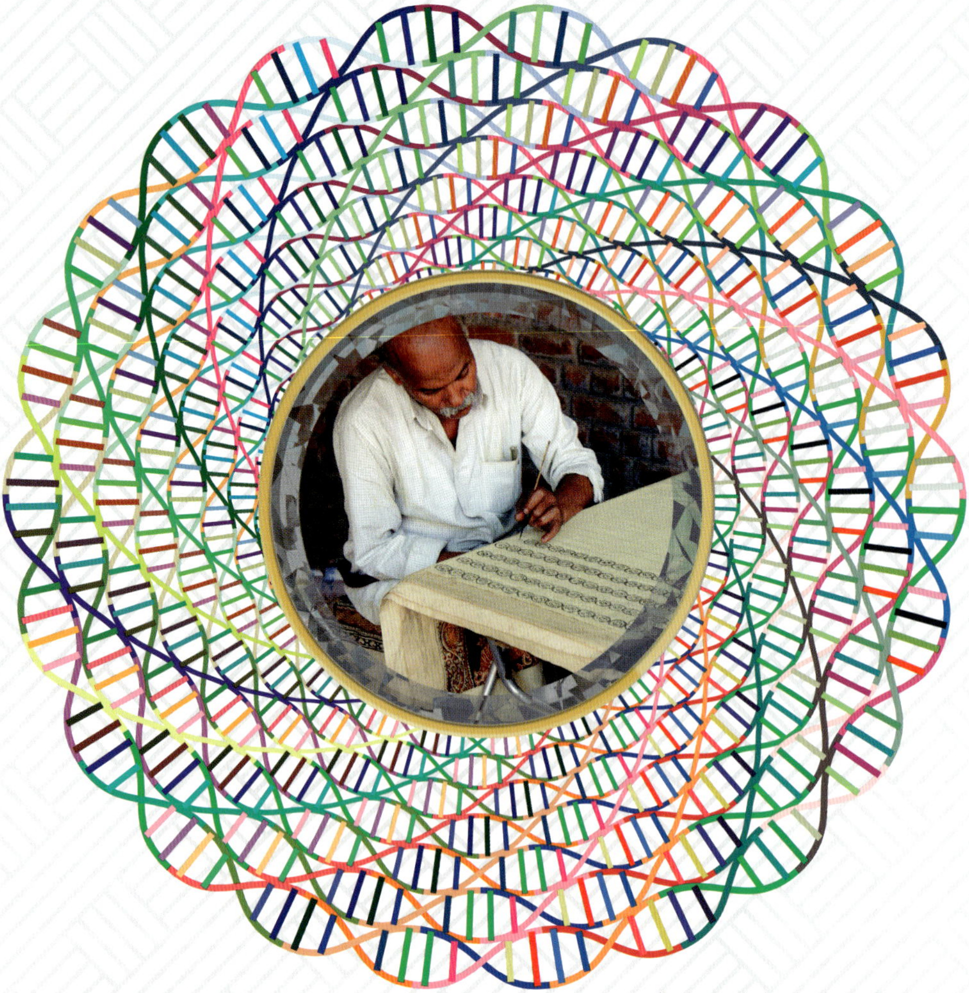

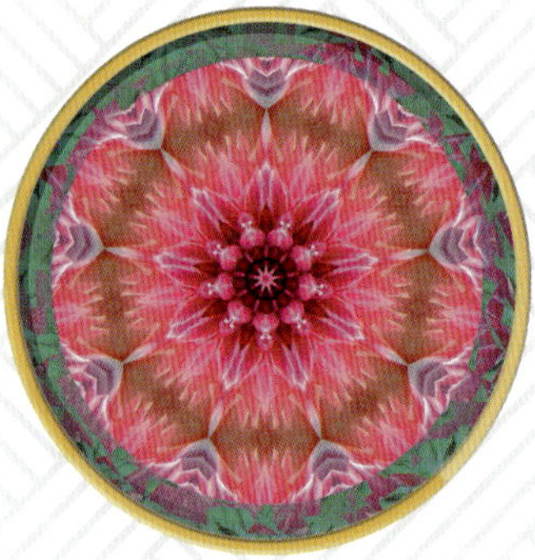

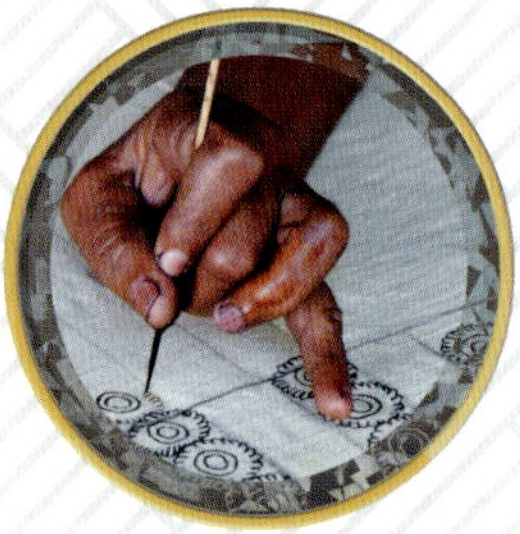

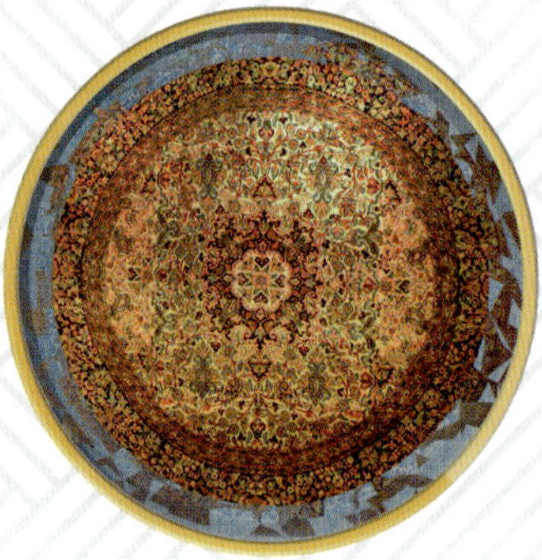

CHAPTER 3

STRATEGIC PLANNING

*Designing a Tapestry of
Heirloom Quality*

How does a capital-intensive manufacturing business grow tenfold in just over three decades in the globally competitive industrial fabric market?

The answer to this question can be distilled down to one idea: an effective and sustained strategic planning process.

Since 1980 Seaman Corporation has embraced and implemented an annual strategic planning process. To remain competitive in a globally competitive industrial fabric marketplace, the company has had to invest millions of dollars in capital equipment and plant expansion. Despite this heavy capital investment and challenging marketplace, the company has sustained consistent and remarkably profitable growth. The company is essentially debt-free.

Strategic planning is critical to the long-term sustainability of any organization. It is more than simply developing a plan for the future. Effective strategic planning is more about the *process* than it is about the plan itself. Focusing only on the implementation of the plan itself assumes a static environment. By sustaining an ongoing planning process, the organization can be responsive to the ever-changing and dynamic economy.

The process must be continual, with constant evaluation of the key factors affecting the business: changing customer needs, competitive landscape, megatrends, government regulations, and macro-

and microeconomic factors. The leadership of the organization must set the time aside to "work on the business" strategically, not simply "work in the business" tactically.

An effective strategic planning process must be done annually. It will allow time, both on-site and off-site, for the senior management team to have candid, dynamic, and honest discussions about the key strategic issues facing the organization. This focus and level of discussion can best be accomplished by engaging an experienced and objective facilitator to lead the meetings.

In the fall of 2008, Seaman Corporation was in the middle of its strategic planning process for fiscal year 2010. Management had finalized and was implementing a reasonable growth business plan for 2009. Yet in the first quarter of its 2009 fiscal year, the company could see that many of the assumptions in the plan were going to be adversely impacted by the country's financial crisis, later known as the Great Recession. Our fears were confirmed when the sales for the first two quarters of fiscal 2009 were significantly below plan and also below the previous year's revenue.

The management team spent the second quarter trying to better understand the long-term impact the crisis would have on Seaman Corporation. The team quickly realized that when the economy emerged from this recession, the world was going to look quite different. Because the company had already developed a strategic plan for the future, management was able to make necessary cost adjustments that remained in alignment with the long-term strategic objectives of the plan. Rather than ask all departments to reduce their operating costs by 10 percent, management was selective and maintained those investments that supported its long-term strategic initiatives.

Because of this selective and strategic cost-reduction process, growth in sales resumed by the third quarter of the fiscal year, and the fourth-quarter revenue results for 2009 were equivalent to the prerecession fourth quarter results of 2008. In addition, the company continued its thirty-year record of achieving annual profitability.

We were able to successfully navigate the challenges of the 2008 financial crisis because we had developed a road map through our strategic planning process. Although the planned sales forecast did not materialize, the planning process identified those initiatives that were critical to future growth and required continual investment. It also identified the areas where future investment could be appropriately reduced.

Many companies facing the same financial crisis issues delayed the recognition of the impact on their business. These companies ultimately reacted by implementing "across the board" cost reductions in hopes that the economy would ultimately return to "normal." As a result, many of these companies failed to navigate this Great Recession and did not survive. If they did survive, their journey to recovery took much longer.

Strategic planning is the process by which a multigenerational company can effectively measure the changes in the economy, the changes in the marketplace, and the changes in competition and see the impact these challenges will have on its business. An effective strategic planning process allows a company to continually adjust to the ever-changing economic conditions and, as required, reinvent itself to adapt to the dynamics of a global economy. Strategic planning is critical to sustaining the growth of a multigenerational business.

Developing a Strategic Planning Process: The Early Days

Seaman Corporation's experience with strategic planning has been a long journey that ultimately resulted in a creative and robust process that continues to be embraced annually by the management team.

In the early 1980s, at the same time I was professionalizing our HR function, there was a great deal of buzz in the business community about this process called "strategic planning." Much was being written about the subject and I became curious about how to apply strategic planning to my family business.

It was apparent that our focus on growth in product development was episodic. We were working day-to-day to keep the business moving forward, doing what we needed to do to make a profit. We were focused primarily on tactical issues. I was very familiar with this because I was involved with our product development process and the ongoing challenges of trying to respond to customer needs.

My inquisitive research led me to two strategic planning resources. The first was an alumnus of my alma mater, Bowling Green State University. He graduated ten years before I did but had returned to Bowling Green to lead the College of Business executive-in-residence program. I was invited to participate in this program and subsequently learned that this alumnus had a great deal of strategic planning experience in his past career. I invited him to meet with our leadership team to describe his strategic planning experience at Carborundum Company and share his facilitation process.

The second resource was a marketing vice president at Rubbermaid, which was headquartered near our family business and had been a source of my informal benchmarking. He shared the valuable insight that when the leadership team engages in an effective strategic planning process, implementation of the strategies becomes far more effective. There is alignment among the management team. You find yourself as CEO talking shorthand with your team. When you start implementing a new initiative, such as hiring an individual to lead a new product line, management does not ask "why?" because they participated in the planning process and already understand the purpose of the new addition.

I had already found this to be true—in the negative—even at our earliest stages. Because the creation of an HR function was solely my idea, I had several managers question the purpose and true value of this cost addition. Had we realized this need through a strategic planning process, the implementation of this initiative would have been far less challenging.

As with any new industry, many "strategic planning consultants" began to surface, professing their capability to teach and implement this new process. The reality was and is that 90 percent of these consultants will not be effective in the long run. The challenge is to find a resource that not only understands the new business process but, more importantly, also understands how this new process can be uniquely and successfully applied to your business.

Recognizing this fact, the executive team at Seaman Corporation decided that my Bowling Green resource was well suited to facilitate a strategic planning process for our organization. Our initial planning session—though rather informal—immediately validated the value and importance of strategic planning. We were able to focus on our markets, our strengths and weaknesses, and our potential growth opportunities (a rough sort of SWOT analysis). As a result, we quickly converged on a unique product development opportunity—aboveground flexible fuel storage tanks, which would store up to 20,000 gallons of fuel to be deployed in combat zones to support our troops' fuel needs.

Flexible above ground pillow tanks utilized for fuel storage at a military fuel depot in Iraq.

The new fabric to make the tanks would replace the more expensive and heavier rubber-based materials traditionally used by the military. The new material would be unlike any we had ever manufactured. Instead of vinyl, the coating polymer had to be urethane to provide the chemical resistance to the various stored fuels. While we had not yet produced a commercial fabric of this nature, our R&D

manager was convinced that it could be produced on the hot-melt coating technology platform we had developed over the past decade.

Because this opportunity was highlighted in our first strategic planning session, the entire management team quickly recognized the potential. The entire team also understood the development challenges and the customer support requirements without the need for months of conversations. Our organizational alignment focused on the commercialization challenges and we were able to expedite a successful solution to this customer's needs.

Over the next several decades, and with the requirements of these tanks needed to support our military operations in the Middle East, this newly developed fabric contributed tens of millions of dollars in sales revenue and business growth. Further development work created an enhanced urethane-coated fabric for flexible fuel storage tanks that have a capacity of more than 200,000 gallons.

The Value of the Process

These early years of strategic planning followed a very basic format. I remained committed to investing management time in this planning process on an annual basis.

I very quickly learned the importance of using an outside resource to facilitate the planning process. This objective third party was in a position to ask questions that internal resources would not be able to voice in the same way. An internal resource might be afraid to ask the tough questions, might put other team members on the defensive, or might be perceived as having a personal agenda.

A quality outside facilitator keeps the process more objective and honest, both in the questions being asked as well as in the responses from the participants. A quality resource will not only keep management more objective but will elevate the quality of strategic thinking by the team as well.

We were fortunate to select this original resource from Bowling Green. He worked with me in advance to determine the meeting agenda. He was quick to understand the nature of our business. He knew how to ask challenging questions in a nonthreatening way—and was not afraid to ask the tough questions.

A major insight I gained from these early years of strategic planning is that *the plan is far less important than the process itself.* That is why it is so important to do the strategic planning on an annual basis. The dynamic nature of the global economy is constantly challenging the assumptions upon which a quality plan is based.

As I said, our early strategic plans were very basic, if not somewhat elementary. The goal of our annual strategic planning cycle was to have a multiyear business plan to guide the future direction of the company and to have a budget for the upcoming year. We did not create a professional looking document only to be placed on a bookshelf.

I became less concerned about the quantitative goals in the plan and more focused on the planning process itself. What were the process initiatives and the organizational requirements necessary to implement the plan? I had the confidence that if these components of the plan were effectively implemented, the quantitative goals would ultimately be achieved.

While we did not always achieve our quantitative goals in the forecasted time period, the planning process itself enhanced the performance of the organization. Engaging in the strategic planning process on an annual basis assured alignment of the leadership team and resulted in more effective business plan execution.

We used our original resource for strategic planning for many years. In fact, I nominated him for our board of directors. His active participation on the board helped educate our outside board members and bring them into alignment with our planning process and the strategic objectives of the company.

Tactical Work Versus Strategic Work

A major challenge to strategic planning is this: How do you protect the long-term strategic work from the short-term tactical work? After several years of using this strategic planning process, we came to the realization that our annual planning process was actually more tactical than strategic. Since our objective was to accomplish a budget for the upcoming business year, we gravitated more to the tactical issues affecting the next year rather than the longer-term strategic issues.

A typical planning session would be to travel off-site for two to three days with little advance preparation other than an established agenda. We spent much of our time trying to understand the marketplace and identify market opportunities. A great deal of that time, though, was spent debating the size of the market, the size and nature of our competition, and the perceived requirements of our customers. We were not coming close to achieving an articulated long-term strategy for the company.

So, at this point, we made a deliberate decision to separate the tactical business year planning from the longer-term strategic planning process. With our fiscal year beginning on October 1, we completed the business plan for the upcoming year by August. Consequently, we decided to begin a true strategic planning process three months into the new fiscal year when we could stay focused on long-term strategic issues facing the company.

At the same time, we decided to invest more time in advance to prepare for the strategic planning off-site session, particularly with market research. In the months leading up to that session, our marketing department updated the studies that defined our markets and their size, our market share, and our competition. We reviewed this information with our sales and management teams in advance of the planning session to confirm that we were in agreement regarding the market and customer data.

A natural outcome of these market reviews was the identification of such strategic issues as these:

- How do we increase our share in an existing market?
- Do we invest in more sales resources?
- Do we invest in social media marketing?
- Do we have opportunities to sell into international markets?
- If so, which countries should we address first?

- What is the best way to penetrate/distribute into those countries?
- Do we need to improve/upgrade our ERP (enterprise resource planning) platform?
- What are the cost-effective options for our company?

We prioritized these issues and selected five to six strategic issues for our team to focus on this planning cycle. Teams of managers were assigned to research these issues further and to develop a set of strategic options.

We specifically avoided focusing on the tactical issues at these sessions, such as addressing the needs of a particular customer or discussing the operating budget for the upcoming year.

As our planning process evolved through the years, we significantly enhanced our strategic discussions by pursuing more formalized SWOT (strengths, weaknesses, opportunities, threats) analyses. We subsequently studied Michael Porter's "Five Forces" framework and applied that analysis to our market reviews.[20] Utilizing these tools in the planning process elevated the strategic thinking of our management team.

Because we had developed consensus around our markets, competition, and customers, we were able to remain focused on the various strategic options during our two-day off-site session each year. This allowed the management team to have productive discussions regarding the strategic challenges facing the company and converge on a strategic direction. At the end of the two days, we had the basics of a three- to five-year strategic business plan.

Over the next two months we had several follow-up sessions during which we finalized a strategic plan that included a detailed sales growth forecast, which then became the basis for our three- to five-year financial forecast, including capital investment requirements. As I mentioned in the section called "Aligning the HR Function with Strategic Objectives" in the previous chapter, at the end of this planning process we also conducted our SEA Session, the driving force of our human capital management process. (This is accomplished with the excellent work done by our HR department, which compiles a very thorough database on all our management associates.)

We asked the crucial questions: Do we have the right organization to drive the strategies in the plan we just completed? Do we have the right people in the right roles at the right time? Several months after completing this strategic planning process, our management team turned its attention to the upcoming annual business plan and operational budget. Because they participated in the recently completed strategic planning process (and the SEA Session), the more tactical annual business plan was developed in alignment with the longer term strategic objectives of the company.

We begin this business planning process approximately seven months into our fiscal year. During May we develop an operational budget. In June we conduct another SEA Session that focuses on the human resource needs for the coming year. In July we finalize the annual business plan for the upcoming fiscal year that begins in October.

An important part of our strategic business planning process is to schedule one day in August to present the plan. We invite all our salaried personnel to attend plus our board of directors and our professional advisers—legal, insurance, financial, and other consultants. At this meeting, we present current year results compared to plan. We present the major strategic initiatives from our strategic planning process. We then present the business plan for the upcoming fiscal year.

This one-day session aligns the entire organization and increases the management team's ability to execute the business plan effectively. It also allows our professional advisers to gain a better understanding of the future direction of the company and thereby improves the quality of service they provide us.

Our annual strategic business planning process—a never-ending leadership and management process—is expressed graphically in the infinity diagram that follows.

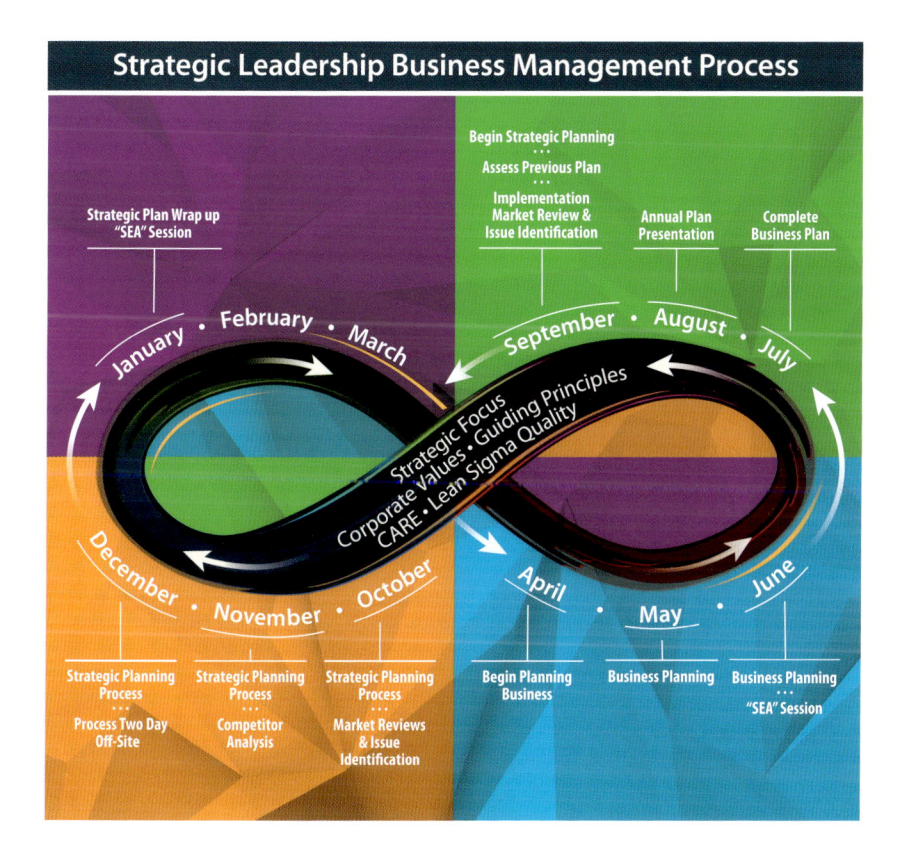

Strategic Leadership Business Management Process

Begin Strategic Planning
- Assess Previous Plan
- Implementation Market Review & Issue Identification
- Annual Plan Presentation
- Complete Business Plan

Strategic Plan Wrap up "SEA" Session

January • February • March — September • August • July

Strategic Focus • Guiding Principles
Corporate Values • Lean Sigma Quality
CARE

December • November • October — April • May • June

Strategic Planning Process
- Process Two Day Off-Site
- Competitor Analysis
- Market Reviews & Issue Identification

Begin Planning Business — **Business Planning** — **Business Planning "SEA" Session**

Although my management team was concerned about the amount of time consumed in meetings that this new strategic and business planning process required, they quickly realized its value and how it supported their ability to carry out their functional responsibilities each year.

As mentioned earlier, there are many reasons to have a quality outside resource facilitate the organization's strategic planning process. One important reason is to raise the level of strategic thinking by the organization.

Most successful organizations have excellent management teams. But, even though these managers are very good at thinking tactically and executing the agreed-upon tactics, many of them find it difficult to shift from the tactical to the strategic. If they are asked to provide a strategic plan for their business unit, the result will most often be a short-term tactical plan. Using a quality outside resource to facilitate the process will elevate the management team's tactical thinking to higher-level strategic thinking.

The Building Blocks of Your Strategic Plan

Most strategic planning resources ask an organization to begin by creating a mission statement. I, myself, resisted this suggestion. In the early stages of strategic planning, the soul-searching an organization does will better define the mission of the company. A mission statement with more integrity will *evolve* from this process rather than initially lead the process.

"Oh no, not someone else with a mission statement."

A strategic planning process consists of many important components. When you begin the process, you must understand your business environment for your business. You need to identify your "true" capabilities—not your desired capabilities. You also need to understand the competitive environment—"Know thy competition." You need to understand and acknowledge your strengths and weaknesses compared to your competitors in the marketplace. You develop this understanding through answering questions such as these:

- What is the macroeconomic environment?
- How will the current domestic economy affect your business?
- How will the global economy affect your business?
- How will government policies affect your business?
- How will societal, demographic, and cultural trends affect your business?
- What do you need to do to protect your existing markets?
- Do you want to remain in those markets over the long term?
- What are future market opportunities?
- What are the barriers to success in those markets?
    - products and service development
    - distribution
    - competition
    - customer perception of their needs

Next, develop the strategies and tactics to maximize the market growth opportunities. Develop a three- to five-year strategic business plan that has specific metrics whereby you can measure your progress and ultimate success.

Once you develop such a multiyear strategic business plan, you will then evaluate your organizational capacity to execute the plan. Do you have the right people on the bus and are they in the right seats?

The annual business plan is developed in alignment with this strategic business plan. It is then monitored on a monthly basis to track both the progress of the plan as well as the assumptions on which the plan is based.

Strategic planning is the heartbeat of a growing company that desires to sustain itself over future generations. Strategic planning provides many benefits to the organization and to its management team. The management team knows the committed direction of the company. The management team can speak shorthand—the team understands why decisions are being made, particularly those that support new initiatives.

A robust strategic planning process is critical to sustaining the growth of a multigenerational business. Sustainable businesses must continually measure the changes in the economy, changes in their marketplace, changes in competition, and the impact these challenges will have on their businesses. Strategic planning is the process that a leadership team utilizes to continually adjust to these ever-changing economic conditions and, if required, reinvent itself to navigate the challenges of a global economy.

Strategic planning is more about the process than the plan itself. Consequently, the planning process should be done on an annual basis and be facilitated by a qualified outside resource. Effective leadership teams should be willing to have their strategic process challenged by a competent outside resource. Such a resource will also assure that management contributes at a strategic level and not simply provide tactical input.

Strategic planning is the primary process that takes the kaleidoscope of pattern choices and designs the tapestry of heirloom quality. The planning process helps refine the vision for this colorful work of art. The process involves the weavers in the design of the tapestry and evaluates their capabilities. By involving the weavers in the process, the entire organization understands and embraces this unique creation. This process will also identify and define the DNA of your business, a key to its lasting legacy.

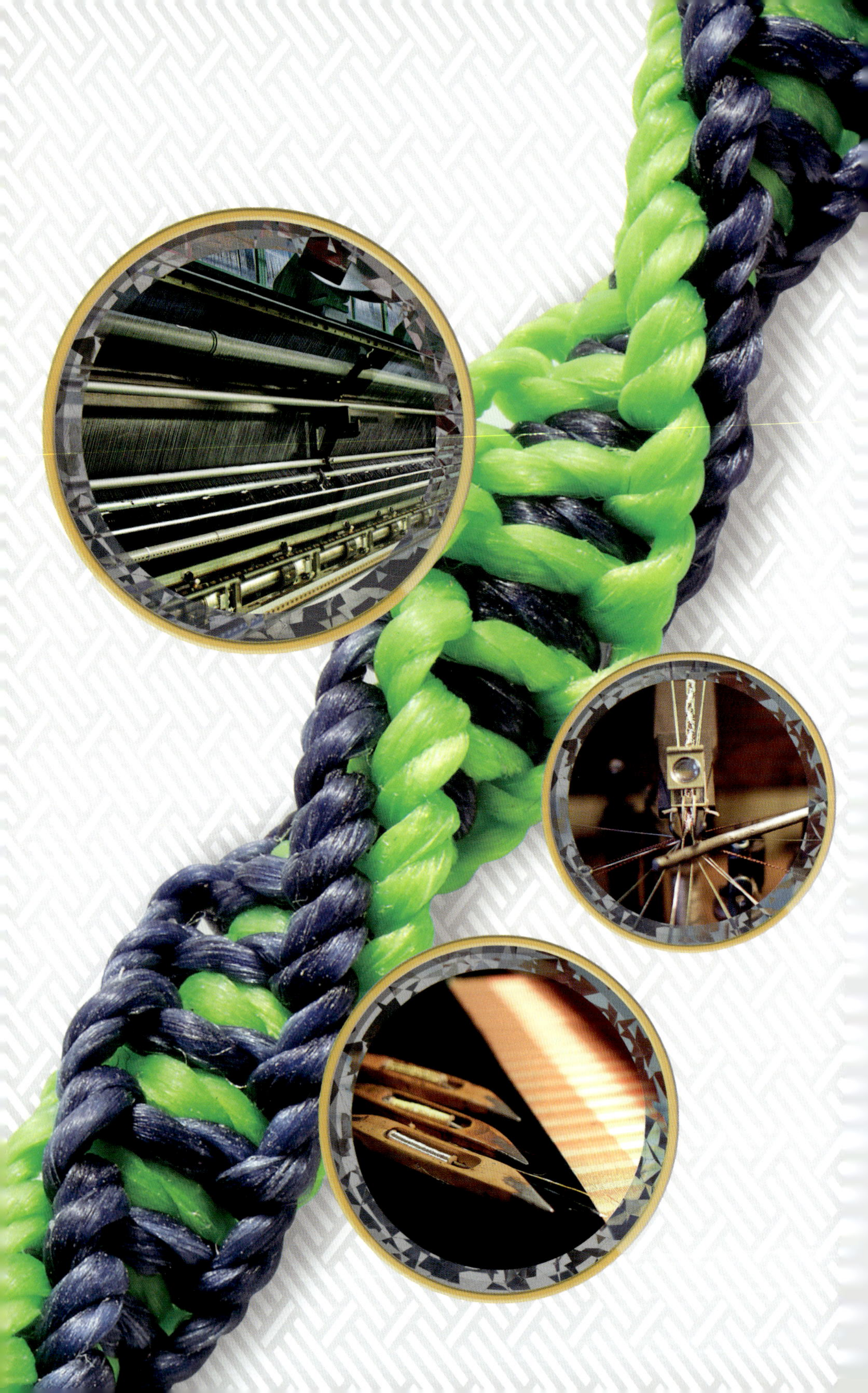

CHAPTER 4

CUSTOMER-FOCUSED QUALITY

Weaving the Tapestry of Heirloom Quality

The long-term sustainability of a business organization is directly related to its ability to continue to provide quality products and service to its customer base.

With the ever-changing business environment, the global competitive marketplace, and the disruption caused by product and service innovation, a multigenerational business must have processes that continually focus on customers' needs to meet their product and service expectations. Businesses that do not meet their customers' ever-changing needs will fail to survive the current generation, let alone be capable of being multigenerational.

My father and mother had a high school education. Nonetheless, as they were building our business, they understood the importance of meeting customer needs. After my father developed a vinyl coating for nylon fabrics, he built his own jury-rigged coating line. The first year of production, he coated 16,000 yards of truck tarp fabric, which he sold to a local tarp manufacturer. During the first year of exposure, however, all that fabric failed.

My father discovered the formulation problem: He had failed to include an ultraviolet light inhibitor. Because of his innate commitment to customer quality, he corrected the problem and decided to replace the entire 16,000 yards—one year of production's worth—at no cost to the customer. Hence, the cornerstone for customer quality at Seaman Corporation was laid.

I, too, learned the lesson of customer quality—in an even more dramatic fashion. My parents sent me off to college to get an education in business management and assumed that I would then add a great deal of value to the family business. They expected me to return with all the answers needed to run and grow the business.

I had gained real-world experience by working in the business throughout my high school and college years. Then, in 1968, I graduated with honors from Bowling Green State University with an undergraduate degree in industrial management and a master's degree in business administration.

I was ready to assume my full-time responsibilities as Plant Manager, responsible for our day-to-day production. I took my job seriously and measured my success by the daily, weekly, and monthly production results.

Our industrial fabrics business produced materials for a variety of outdoor heavy-duty applications, predominantly for the truck tarp industry. We began by weaving specialized fabrics and processing them through a series of coating lines. We had a number of customers scattered throughout the United States who would buy these fabrics to fabricate into truck tarps.

Our largest customer was in Dallas, Texas, representing approximately 10 percent of our annual sales. I worked hard in overseeing the production and shipment of their order requirements. In several shipments there were some minor weaving defects in our base fabric, but these defects affected only the aesthetic quality of the material and not the functional purpose of the fabric—namely, to remain waterproof and to protect cargo on a truck trailer. Because I thought these fabrics would still maintain the performance characteristics required by our customer—that is, not leak—I was not overly concerned about shipping fabric that had a few minor aesthetic or appearance defects.

During this period, my father was spending most of his time at our Florida manufacturing facility. We would talk daily about production. Periodically, he would return to our Ohio operation.

When he began hearing complaints from our Texas customer through our sales manager, he suggested that I make a trip with him to visit the customer, which I was certainly willing to do. But when my father called our largest customer to arrange a visit, the customer told him it would be a waste of our time because he had just placed all his fabric business with our major competitor!

So, there I was—an honors graduate with two business degrees—and my first major accomplishment was losing our largest customer. Quality *is* in the eye of the beholder, I learned. Quality is not defined by the company who produces the product, regardless of its performance capability. The product I was shipping for truck tarps did not meet all the fabric requirements our customer expected, aesthetics included.

While painful and expensive at the time, this experience was certainly one of the most valuable lessons I learned early in my career. I vowed to never let production and shipping pressures compromise the high quality our customers expected of our products.

Product Quality Depends on Employee Engagement

Many years later I learned another very important lesson about product quality and service. If your organization is going to sustain a culture of customer-focused product and service quality, every associate in your business must be actively engaged in the quality-improvement process.

As described in the chapter on "Human Capital," in 1987 Seaman Corporation relocated our Millersburg, Ohio, manufacturing plant twenty-five miles north to Wooster. After several months in this new facility with its upgraded equipment, we found that our production output decreased and our product quality declined.

Once again, experience taught me a very valuable lesson. Despite the company having made a significant capital investment in a new plant and in upgraded equipment, our associates, whose jobs we had saved, felt so disenchanted that they wanted a union to represent their interests. After listening to their concerns, I recognized that to invest in property, plant, and equipment was not sufficient for running a business. Investments must also be made in your human capital.

We responded to our associates' concerns with a strong communications program in an effort to assure them that we were serious about addressing these concerns. Fortunately, we were successful in achieving a vote of confidence during the union election process. Following this election success, I immediately began exploring current business processes that addressed product quality and associate engagement.

Earlier in the 1980s the success that Dr. W. Edwards Deming had in revolutionizing Japan's manufacturing industries was being recognized and adopted by American industry. We were fortunate to find the Hertz Group, a consulting company led by Paul Hertz, who had studied under Dr. Deming and was endorsed to teach his philosophy and his business principles.

After understanding the Deming principles, it became apparent that we would need to make a significant investment in the training and development of our associates. We began with our leadership team and our supervisors. This was followed by multiday training sessions for all our associates in groups of twenty-five to thirty over a period of several months. Together, those steps represented a significant capital and time investment by the company, all focused on our human resources.

The successful implementation of the Deming principles required a major change in our management philosophy. When management identified problem issues, instead of telling the associates how to resolve them, they were now to actively engage these associates to help identify, develop, and implement solutions.

We realized that our associates and the company wanted to achieve the same result—provide quality product and service to our customers. If we failed to accomplish this objective, we would not remain in business. We also learned that the most effective way to solve a production or quality problem was to positively engage the associates who were involved in producing that product or service.

Developing a Unique Quality Initiative Process: CARE

A major component of our quality journey was to explore a variety of other quality-initiative processes. We benchmarked companies like Milliken & Company and New United Motors Manufacturing, Incorporated (NUMMI), a joint venture between General Motors and Toyota.

The NUMMI story was a great testament to the potential of a robust quality-initiative process. The Oakland, California, GM plant was the worst assembly plant in the company's facilities in the 1980s. A plant manager would last about a year. The assembly line workers were under strong United Autoworkers protection, and it was rumored that you could purchase on the assembly line floor literally anything illegal that you desired.

GM subsequently closed the plant. Several years later, they partnered with Toyota to reopen the plant utilizing the Deming management principles. They had to get the approval of the UAW to reopen this facility. The union agreed as long as NUMMI promised to rehire all the previous workers.

GM and Toyota agreed to do so, but only on the condition that all the supervisors and workers go through the Toyota training program before the reopening. Following this extensive training, the plant reopened and soon became the highest-quality production facility in the GM system.

We also studied the work of other quality consultants, such as Phil Crosby, and we evaluated the requirements of the Malcolm

Baldridge National Quality Award, a recognition awarded annually by the US Department of Commerce to US companies that demonstrate high performance quality and service results.

Benchmarking provided a vast amount of information to our organization about how to implement sustainable quality-initiative programs. Nevertheless, this process also seemed to send a confusing message to our associates. Are we doing Deming? Are we implementing Crosby principles? Is this the Milliken way? What is the Malcolm Baldridge National Quality Award?

Because I had spent considerable time learning about each of these quality approaches, I was able to visualize how all these philosophies were in alignment. But I was also able to see that at the supervisor and worker levels it could seem very confusing.

So, I decided to take a multiday retreat, review what I had learned during the past twelve to eighteen months, and attempt to author a quality-initiative process that was unique to Seaman Corporation. After developing distinct quality practice principles, I reviewed them with my senior management team and further revised the principles of our process. While these principles align with the Malcolm Baldridge evaluation criteria, they became uniquely the quality process for Seaman Corporation and our associates.

To sustain a quality-initiative process, we needed an identity. We selected the term CARE because it became the acronym that conveyed our two primary purposes:

Customers Are the Reason for Excellence
our external focus

Competitive Advantage Requires Excellence
our internal focus

Our CARE philosophy became the guiding principles for how we conducted business at Seaman Corporation on a day-to-day basis. It focused on quality and service as perceived in the eyes of the customer.

CARE

Customers Are the Reason for Excellence
- Leadership
- 100% Total Customer Satisfaction
- Quality

Competitive Advantage Requires Excellence
- Strategic Quality Planning
- Human Resource Planning
- Quality Assurance of 100% Total Customer Satisfaction
- System and Measurements

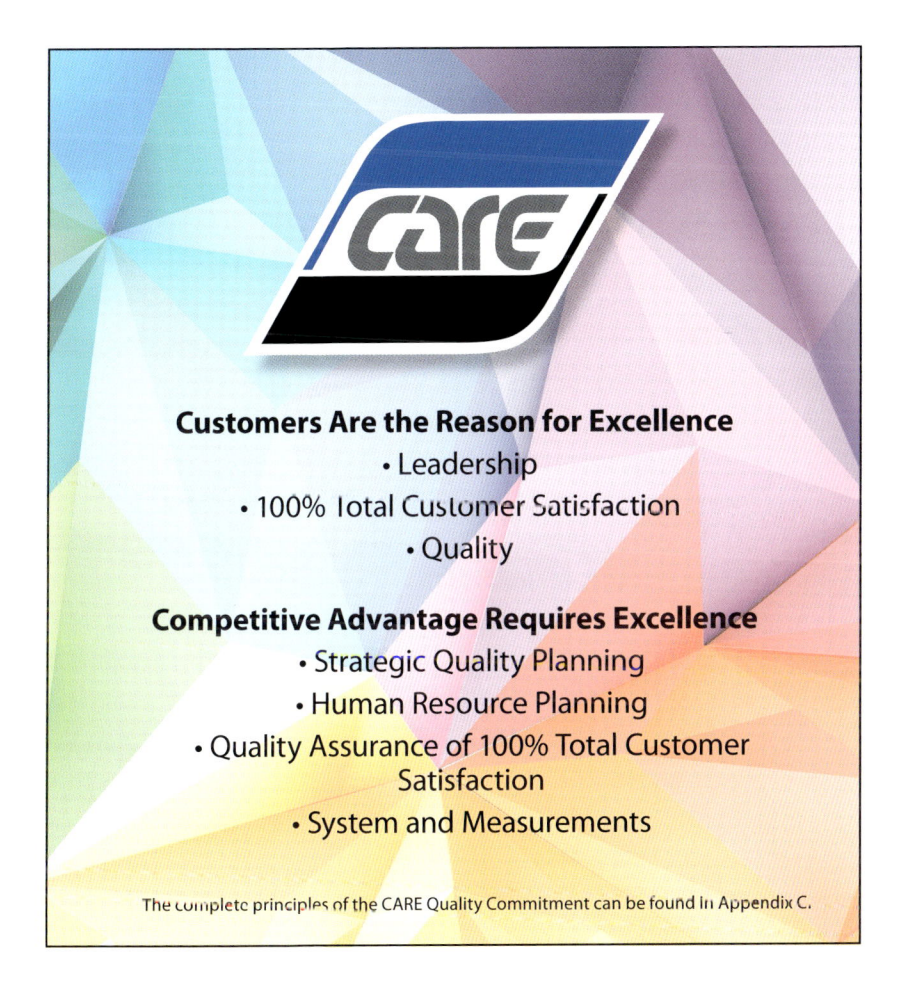

The complete principles of the CARE Quality Commitment can be found in Appendix C.

Sustainable Quality Initiative Processes Require Commitment

The success of a change initiative of this magnitude requires the visible leadership and active involvement of the CEO and the senior management team. Otherwise, the effort will be perceived as the "program of the month" and elicit sarcastic responses such as, "This, too, shall pass."

I have observed many CEOs enthusiastically introduce a major quality change initiative but then expect their staff to do the implementation. When the CEO changed focus and was not seen "walking the talk," the quality principles would slowly fade away and the organization would return to "business as usual." Successfully institutionalizing quality-initiative principles in any organization requires a significant investment in both money and senior management leadership time.

Sustainability of a customer-focused quality process is very challenging. Day-to-day business activity will compete with the sustained implementation of these principles. Leadership must find a way to showcase the quality principles daily.

A major part of institutionalizing our CARE Quality Commitment was to showcase our process to our customers. Once I felt we were well on the way to implementing CARE, I invited customers to our manufacturing facilities and presented the CARE principles to them. I made these presentations with our management team present.

When I first suggested bringing customers to visit, our sales staff were very hesitant. They were convinced that customers would focus on pricing issues and try to negotiate lower prices.

To the contrary, once the CARE presentation was made and a plant tour was given, rarely did a customer raise the topic of pricing. In fact, I found that customers wanted to be partners with a company that was so focused on the levels of quality they expected, and they wanted to emulate us in their own businesses. Making CARE presentations not only kept the principles alive in our organization but also proved to be one of the most effective ways to build strong sustainable customer relationships.

Evolving the Quality Initiative

Our CARE Quality Initiative principles continue to guide how we run our company. The continual implementation of these principles clearly differentiates us from our competition with our customers. They keep our organization focused on our customers and their ever-changing needs. Associates who do not have direct contact with the customers who buy our products realize that they have an internal customer—namely, the downstream departments in Seaman

Corporation. The better job they do serving their internal customer with quality, the better the organization will do in serving the external customers' needs.

A customer-focused quality improvement program consists of many components, as expressed in the seven principles of our CARE Quality Commitment.

Customers Are the Reason for Excellence includes:
- leadership
- 100 percent total customer satisfaction
- continuous quality improvement

Competitive Advantage Requires Excellence includes:
- strategic quality planning
- HR development
- quality assurance
- systems and measurements

The attention to customer support and service requires investment and can add costs to the organization. Consequently, one of the metrics of our CARE process is the "cost of quality."

An organization can deliver on many of the quality principles and deliver only top-quality product and services. But, if there is not an equal focus on reducing the cost of quality, the product and service will not be competitive. Conversely, reducing the cost of quality through a philosophy of never-ending improvement can actually make the delivery of quality products and services more competitive. This culture of never-ending improvement is a key component to creating a sustainable organization.

As Seaman Corporation continued to grow through the successful implementation of our CARE Quality Commitment process, it became increasingly evident that we were not effectively implementing one of the key principles as part of quality assurance: the cost of quality.

We were doing an excellent job of shipping only first-grade quality fabrics to our customers on time. Our first-run yield—a key cost-of-quality metric—however, was consistently in the 90–92 percent range. That meant that 8–10 percent of the product we were producing was classified as "offgrades." As the company grew, this became a multimillion-dollar component of our cost-of-quality metrics.

In 2005, I challenged our management leadership to address this factor. I asked them to explore and identify the best processes for attacking production-quality issues. I knew this would require a company-wide effort and a significant investment, similar to the CARE Quality Initiative process we developed years before. I wanted this to be led by senior leadership and not perceived as another new program that came out of the CEO's office.

Management leadership identified and evaluated a number of quality improvement processes that were being utilized in manufacturing environments. They converged on Lean Sigma as the leading-edge quality improvement process. Lean Sigma combines the Toyota principles of lean manufacturing—eliminating non-value-added activities from processes—with Six Sigma, the Deming statistical control measurement discipline. After evaluating several potential consulting candidates, the team recommended TBM Consulting to be our partner in this new initiative.

It is worth noting why TBM Consulting was selected. This consulting company had been successfully implementing Lean Sigma programs in a wide variety of businesses, both manufacturing and service, for more than twenty years. They provided a unique and intensive training process. They insisted that we communicate to our associates that there would be no workforce layoffs as a result of efficiency gains from the Lean Sigma events.

Once again, we trained all our associates in these Lean Sigma principles. We then began attacking our quality and productivity challenges utilizing the TBM Lean Sigma approach. We had associates who were involved in the production or service processes leave their normal workstations and spend a week focused on improving the identified business challenge.

TBM also had a novel way of facilitating each weeklong "Lean" event. The event would start on Monday with a detailed description of how the process currently worked. By midweek, ideas for improving the process were being evaluated. Then, in the final days of the week, these ideas had to be actually implemented.

This allowed the associates to immediately see the value of their ideas put into action. It did not take too many Lean events before our associates began to feel that they were actually engaged in the improvement process and were making a significant contribution. This process became an effective way to tap into the ideas and input from all our associates. It also provided the associates with a deep sense of personal accomplishment. And, if the efficiencies and quality gains resulted in fewer jobs in the work process, those associates were redeployed to focus on other process-improvement opportunities.

Continuing to use TBM as our consultant has enabled us to sustain our Lean Sigma initiative. TBM does an annual audit to determine how well we are institutionalizing the principles and maintaining the quality and productivity gains. They also help us identify additional opportunities for Lean events, and we commit to five or six such events at each manufacturing facility per year. Many of these events are now focused on our business processes. Lean Sigma requires that we sustain our never-ending improvement culture.

The commitment to Lean Sigma principles over the last decade has helped us achieve significant improvements. Our first-run yield now averages 97 percent, resulting in more than $35 million of direct savings over the past thirteen years. In addition to reducing waste, Lean Sigma has increased the capability of our manufacturing and business processes. Productivity has improved from 72 percent to 82 percent. On-time delivery increased from 88 percent to 96 percent, and inventory turns went from 4.0 to an average of 8.8 over the past ten years. This increased capacity and flexibility allows us to better meet the changing demands of the marketplace and our customers.

Our commitment to Lean Sigma and the success we achieved in sustaining the implementation of these principles resulted in TBM awarding Seaman Corporation the "Perfect Engine Award" in 2012, presented annually to a company that demonstrates success in implementing LeanSigma statistics-based quality and efficiency improvement. This award represents a significant accomplishment on the part of all the Seaman associates who are actively engaged in our culture of never-ending improvement.

Perfect Engine Award

Measuring Customer and Employee Satisfaction

A customer-focused product and service quality process is critical to sustaining the growth of a business organization over time. Our ever-changing global market environment will always create competitive pressures and impact the needs of customers. A growing business will continually expose the Achilles heels within an organization.

These process-improvement opportunities can best be identified in their early stages by constantly engaging customers *and* associates. This is best accomplished by conducting regular customer satisfaction surveys and associate satisfaction surveys.

Collecting customer satisfaction surveys on an annual basis provides current objective feedback about product and service quality and your performance relative to your competitors. Similarly, distributing associate satisfaction surveys on a regular basis can quickly identify dissatisfaction, poor supervision of departments, misalignment with company goals, and other "red flags" that need to be quickly addressed. The surveys help customers and associates alike feel engaged in the decisions that are being made to run the business.

The long-term sustainability of a business organization is directly dependent on its ability to provide quality products and services to its customers. A business must define quality as seen through the eyes (and ears) of the customer. A customer-focused quality-initiative process is required for the entire organization to recognize these changing customer needs and to address them in a timely and competitive manner.

The principles of a process like Lean Sigma will keep the focus on never-ending improvement of all the business processes. Lean Sigma is like a pebble tossed into the pond, with far-reaching ripples that reduce waste and increase capability throughout the organization.

A customer-focused quality business will regularly conduct customer surveys to gather objective feedback on how well the organization is meeting their needs, particularly compared to the competition. It will also do employee surveys to determine how well management is communicating and supporting the employees in accomplishing customer satisfaction at all levels. The business will use quality processes such as Lean Sigma to continually improve all the business processes that support cost-efficient customer quality.

The success of any such quality-initiative process is directly related to the active engagement of the organization's CEO and the leadership team. The quality process requires daily involvement of all associates. This commitment to implementing these quality principles on a sustainable basis requires visible leadership support at all levels of the organization.

A woven rug becomes a tapestry because its level of quality has been sustained over many generations. Part of this quality is a result of the materials selected and the equipment used in the original creation of the tapestry. But the enduring heirloom quality of the tapestry is a direct function of the artistic talent and capability of the many weavers who will execute the tapestry's design. Investing in the weavers of your organization to keep them customer-focused and committed to never-ending improvement is vital to creating a multigenerational business organization of heirloom quality.

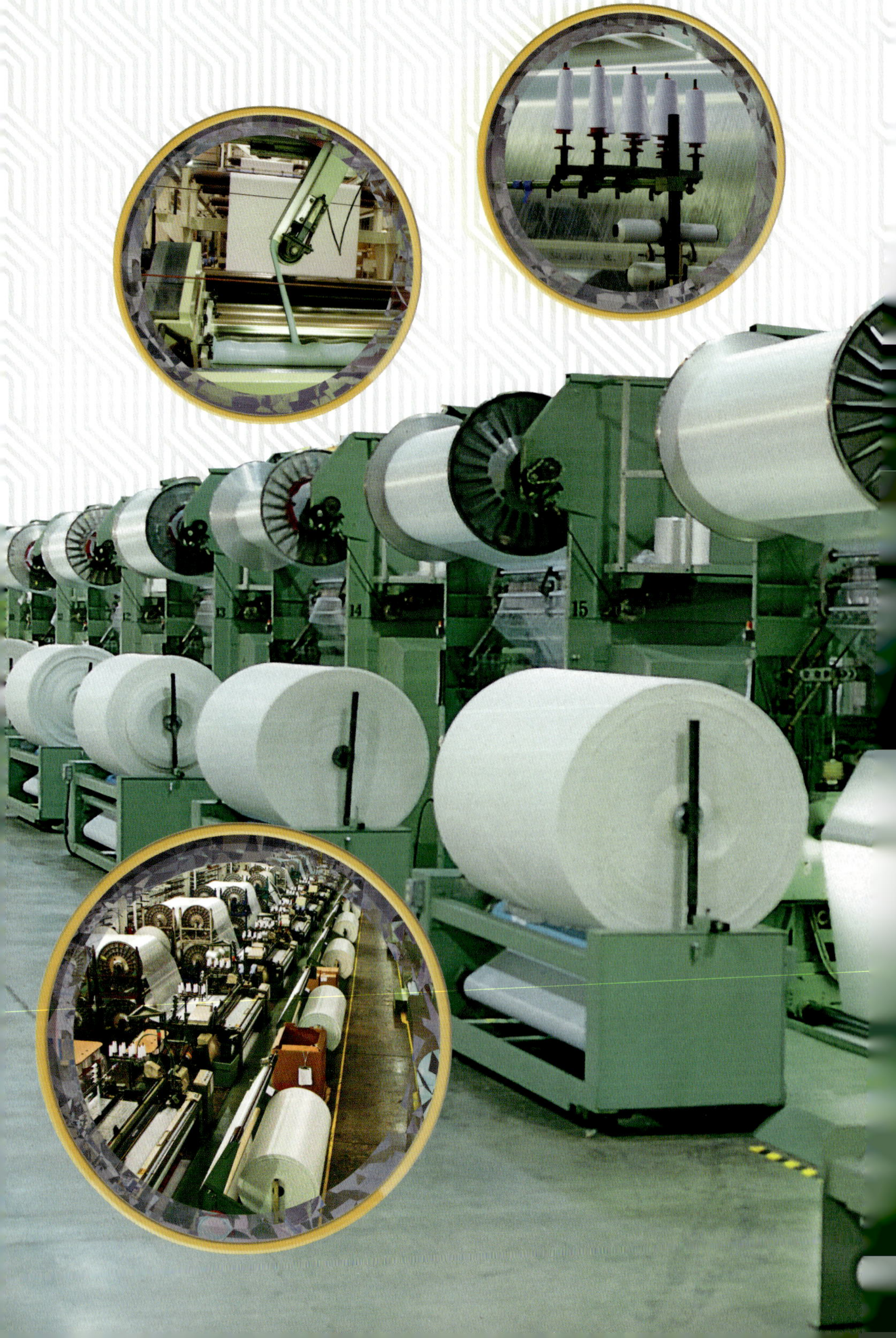
14
15

CHAPTER 5

A STRATEGIC IMPERATIVE

*Creating Heirloom Quality
Through Constant Reinvestment*

> *"Richard, you have only two choices. You either make this
> investment . . . or you sell the company!"*

These were the words of Teresa Amabile, a Harvard Business School faculty member and long-time Seaman Corporation board member. It was our March 2001 board meeting. For this and several board meetings prior, we had focused on evaluating the largest single capital investment in the history of the company.

To make this decision even more complex, if we committed to this investment, the equipment would be purchased in Europe and it would take two years to design, build, ship, install, and get it "up and running" in our Ohio manufacturing plant.

Teresa's words captured the essence of committing to the strategic imperative of continual reinvestment. If your desire is to "harvest" your business sometime in the future, or if your business objective is to support your lifestyle, then continual reinvestment will not be a strategic imperative. If, however, you want to build a foundation for a business that will be in existence a hundred years from now, continual reinvestment is vital.

Why does a multigenerational business require continual reinvestment? First, as a growing enterprise, the business will need to invest in additional capacity. But, more importantly, it will need to reinvest to meet the challenges of an ever-changing economy and the impact that change will have on customer needs.

The technology platforms upon which your business is based are constantly undergoing slight modifications. Competitive challenges come from many global fronts where, in some cases, state-sponsored subsidies fund the latest equipment and service technology of your foreign competitors. Reinvestment is necessary to stay ahead of both curves.

Seaman Corporation has time and again recognized the importance of reinvestment. The company my father created was in the industrial textile business. In the early 1950s, nylon fabrics and vinyl compounding were just emerging. The development work he did (in my mother's kitchen, you will recall) might have been considered some of the most innovative in the world. In fact, at the end of that decade, we actually showcased our product at the World's Fair in Moscow, Russia.

Over the course of time, most of that industrial fabric technology and manufacturing capability moved offshore. In fact, when I tell people about our business, the first question they often ask is where do we manufacture our products and from what countries do we import our fabrics. People are stunned when I tell them we are manufacturing in Tennessee and Ohio, and, in fact, we are selling high-performance industrial fabrics *into* China!

This can only have been accomplished because we have a strategic imperative to reinvest in property, plant, equipment, technology, and human capital.

The commitment of successful multigenerational family businesses to the reinvestment imperative is confirmed by the EY 2017 Growth Survey:

> . . . 62% of the [family] businesses said that they have never released equity to a third party in exchange for investment. . . . Two-thirds of the survey respondents say they grow and innovate by investing their own money. And family businesses appear conservative in their willingness to take on debt. . . .

> Being a private family company in control of its investment means they can react quickly as conditions change. They can seize the moment in areas with high potential for growth or make long-term potentially disruptive investments—without answering to public shareholders or outside investors looking for short-term payoffs.[21]

The foundation for a reinvestment culture started early in the history of our company. My father had successfully built coating equipment that applied liquid vinyl and urethane coatings to fabrics. When he learned about another process that was being utilized in Europe, however, he was intrigued. Engineers had designed and built mini-calenders that utilized rotating hot rolls to press solid compounds into sheets of plastic. This hot-melt coating equipment was designed to use less expensive resins to produce vinyl and urethane coatings, though they were not yet commonly applying these coatings to nylon and polyester fabrics.

Although our business at the time was doing just $2 million in annual sales, my father was willing to commit to a *$300,000 investment* to purchase and import hot-melt equipment, creating a technology platform that had never been tried in the United States. He visualized this equipment and technology being able to use resin that was half the cost while also producing more competitive high-performance vinyl- and urethane-coated fabrics.

This equipment was built, shipped, and installed in 1968—coincidentally, the year I graduated from Bowling Green State University with an MBA. That degree did little to prepare me for the next two years of trying to produce a commercial product on this unique technology platform that my father had decided was the future of our industry.

Eventually, we did just that. My father's vision continues to be a reality today. More than 75 percent of the products we manufacture are produced on this technology platform.

Weaving technology is another good example of the value of reinvestment. In the 1960s, we were utilizing conventional weaving equipment that produced variations of the traditional "basket weaves," with the weft yarns interwoven with the warp yarns.

My father learned of another type of equipment, also built in Europe, which produced an industrial fabric by laying the weft yarns on top of the warp yarns and "stitching" them together with a knitting process. This unique fabric-formation process appealed to my father because it not only produced a base fabric three times as fast as traditional weaving; the coated fabric also had much higher tear strength and improved dimensional stretch properties.

Seaman Corporation was the first company in the United States to invest in this equipment. We spent several years with the equipment perfecting a commercial coated fabric. But it was not long before we were investing in the improved weft insertion technology. The base cloths we developed with this technology platform became the standard in many of the industrial fabric markets. These base clothes represent more than 60 percent of the weft-inserted coated fabrics we market and sell today.

Turning Unforeseen Circumstances into Opportunities

If a company supports a strategic imperative to reinvest, it becomes a natural process to continually identify opportunities to increase capacity and be prepared to quickly commit to these investments. As I wrote earlier, family businesses are uniquely inclined to take advantage of these opportunities.

In 1976, one of our major competitors decided to sell its industrial fabric facility in Tennessee. It took us less than a week to negotiate the purchase of their equipment and have the required expansion capability for our growing business.

Because of the nature of our competitor's equipment and other business issues, it took us two years to make this investment productive and profitable. Then, in 1980, we increased our investment by negotiating the purchase of the leased property and plant, which assured our long-term presence at this Tennessee location.

Similarly, as I previously described, in the middle 1980s, our twenty-five-year-old manufacturing plant in Millersburg, Ohio, was suddenly facing an unexpected cost increase in property insurance. Our insurance premium went from $20,000 to $120,000 seemingly overnight, with the distinct possibility that we might be uninsurable in the future. No amount of strategic planning could have prepared us for that challenge, but our culture of reinvestment did help us move forward with potential options.

Should we consolidate with our Tennessee manufacturing facility? That property was landlocked and would limit our future expansion possibilities. Additionally, we would lose more than a hundred associates, many of whom retained the historical knowledge of our company's technology.

Should we make our largest capital investment ever and build a new corporate office and manufacturing plant in Wooster, Ohio, just twenty miles north? While this option was a much higher financial risk and had a much lower short-term ROI, it would preserve the jobs of a hundred knowledgeable associates. With the benefit of input from our outside board of directors, we selected the riskier option and made a significant financial investment in a new manufacturing plant in Wooster.

Oftentimes these types of investments have unforeseen benefits. Within a few months of moving into the new facility, we invited a customer who was developing a new billboard communication product with our fabric to visit our plant. Once he saw our plant and location, he returned a few weeks later and asked us to build a large manufacturing plant for him to lease for his product growth and expansion. This decision helped make him a captive customer for many years.

Additionally, our new facility in Wooster made it much easier to recruit management talent since it was located in a larger and more vibrant community. We are still a proud part of the community today, employing 175 people and leading and participating in a wide variety of community initiatives.

Strategic Planning Drives Proactive Reinvestment

A growing business must constantly be looking at new investment opportunities. As mentioned at the beginning of this chapter, in 2001 we faced a decision to make a significant capital investment or to sell the company. This capital investment was required to upgrade our hot-melt technology platform and the supporting equipment that my father had purchased in 1968.

This new equipment would be wider, operate at higher speeds, and have significantly improved process controls. The investment, however, was fifteen times greater than what my father spent.

> *"Richard, you have only two choices. You either make this investment . . . or you sell the company!"*

While the financial risk seemed ominous, we nonetheless placed a multimillion-dollar purchase order with the Italian company. Two weeks later, 9/11 occurred. With the economic turmoil this attack on the United States created, we obviously revisited and questioned our decision to make this significant capital investment.

We decided to remain committed to this capital project. The equipment was designed, built, and installed on schedule. And, while unforeseen two years earlier when we placed the order, we began operating the new equipment by producing the military fabrics required to support the troops in our overseas military engagements.

Because of the hard work and effort of all our associates, this capital project became one of the best investment decisions in the company's history. In fact, the equipment and technology were so successful at producing our hot-melt coated fabrics that within six months of start-up, we returned to Italy and placed the order for a *second* multimillion-dollar machine to be installed in our Tennessee manufacturing facility.

While these types of investments can appear to be high risk and overwhelming, using a disciplined evaluation process can make them "measured risk" investments. By implementing a robust strategic planning process that captures the input of management leadership and by taking advantage of sharing this evaluation process with an outside board of directors, the seemingly high risk of these investments can be mitigated.

This deliberate evaluation process continually looks at the domestic and international competitive forces and focuses on the capacity and capability of the equipment. At what point do you need to make the investment to support additional capacity? More importantly, where do you need to make additional investment to improve your technology capability? What new technology capabilities do you need to consider?

These types of questions and considerations require time and need to be evaluated proactively so that you are not forced in the face of competition to make a decision reactively. For example, the major investment we made in new wide-width hot-melt coating equipment was under evaluation by our strategic leadership team and our board of directors for more than three years.

Shortly after we invested in two new hot-melt coating lines, we learned that a competitive Chinese industrial fabric company had spent $18 million to purchase similar hot-melt coating equipment and develop the capability to produce similar coated fabrics. My COO and I visited China in 2006 and we were invited to see this Chinese state-owned manufacturing company.

While traveling to the plant outside Shanghai, the general manager turned to me and said, "Mr. Seaman, we know you are the best in the world at producing industrial fabrics with this hot-melt coating technology. We want you to teach us how to produce quality products on our new hot-melt coating equipment so that we can compete in the United States."

While somewhat stunned at this request, I took this as a naive but credible testimony of the value of our sustained investments in this technology platform.

The author and his COO, Jim Dye, visit China in 2006

Committing to a strategic imperative for continual reinvestment and embedding this into the corporate culture helps support rapid decision making when required for capital investments.

When I went to Italy to purchase a second hot-melt coating line, I was told by the supplier that if we wanted to meet my desired shipping date, I would have to commit to the multimillion-dollar purchase within twenty-four hours or the delivery would be extended a year because of another pending order. I was able to contact my board overnight and had their approval in time to place the order the following day.

Similarly, we recently experienced a major disruption in our supply chain for polyester yarn, one of the primary raw materials for our fabrics. Our primary domestic supplier, owned by a private equity firm, called and said they were closing their only US plant in ninety days as a result of selling their other international assets.

Not only did this impact the domestic supply of a major raw material, it also had a dramatic impact on our weaving technology. For decades, our warp yarn was supplied on large section beams by our suppliers. Due to consolidation in the industry, this beaming capability was very limited and now our primary source was closing down.

Because of our history and culture of investment and reinvestment, the leadership team quickly responded to this supply chain disruption. We immediately purchased millions of pounds of yarn inventory from the supplier. In addition, we were the first to commit to purchase the equipment this supplier was selling because it would enable us to develop our own beaming capability. That included hiring some of the experienced talent who were no longer going to have a job.

In addition, we discovered an opportunistic option to purchase a large facility located only two hundred yards from our existing Tennessee manufacturing plant. We were then able to store the inventory and install the beaming operation in a facility located in close proximity to our existing one. Again, because of our culture of reinvestment and our faith in the growth of our business, we responded quickly to these investment opportunities.

Our quick decision-making actions took the entire industry by surprise. This investment in inventory, equipment (and the expertise to use it), technology, and a facility gave us a major competitive advantage, particularly in future military business, where the Berry Amendment requires domestic supply, when available, for the textile products purchased by the Department of Defense.

Investing in Your People

Continual reinvestment cannot be limited to property, equipment, and technology. Equally important is the investment made in human resources.

The growth and development of your associates and your management team will not arise simply because of the compensation paid. If you want to grow your business and you are not growing your associates, business growth will likely not occur. New and younger associates need to be added to your team to allow the company to remain nimble and to better navigate the current changing technology environment. Investments also need to be made in information technology to leverage the talent and capabilities of your associates.

In 2012, it was time to upgrade our twenty-year-old ERP platform. Again, we knew this would require a major capital investment but also would threaten to be a major disruption to the work responsibilities of all our associates. We evaluated many ERP choices and decided to make the investment in Oracle.

At first, we were advised that we were not large enough for their platform and would be spending too much money. Because of our commitment to growth and wanting an IT infrastructure that would support the future, though, we concluded that Oracle was our best investment. (Ironically, it took some convincing on their end to let us purchase and implement their product!)

Because we knew that the conversion to any new ERP system can be very disruptive to the organization and, more importantly, to our customer base, we took two years to prepare for the implementation before going live. It was still a painful and expensive conversion nonetheless. We had to customize the platform, test out the software, and provide everyone with adequate training. If data were added incorrectly or were incomplete, the business order process would not advance.

Fortunately, the investment and proper implementation paid off. We did not disrupt our customers or their businesses. Investing in this major ERP platform has even allowed us to "plug in" other IT platforms such as Saleforce.com.

Today this significant investment in IT platforms provides all our associates with comprehensive, timely information, leveraging their ability to better perform their responsibilities and providing us with a stronger competitive advantage.

Investing as a Multigenerational Family Business

Investments in property, plant, equipment, and future technology represent high financial risks and oftentimes have long-term payoffs. Public companies pressured to focus on short-term earnings shy away from these types of investments. Owners who use their businesses to support their lifestyles avoid these investments. If the business is going to be "harvested" in the future, seldom are these major investments undertaken.

The same is true for private-equity-owned companies. Because the financial strategy of private equity prioritizes paying down the leveraged debt as quickly as possible, most of the cash flow generated is allocated to debt repayment rather than reinvestment in the business. By contrast, companies that want to be multigenerational require a strategic imperative to constantly evaluate and commit to major new investments even if they do not appear to have a short-term payback.

Currently, our company has the capacity to produce 33 percent more sales volume. Therefore, our new investment opportunities are not based on increasing capacity. Nevertheless, investments that help us leverage our technology platforms to manufacture new products for existing or new markets are always under evaluation. For instance, we recently made a $5-million investment in equipment that significantly enhances one of our technology platforms primarily for the purpose of challenging our product and new business development teams to create growth opportunities.

Committing to a strategic imperative for reinvestment has significant implications for a growing family business and its shareholders. A major portion of the earnings is required to fund its ongoing growth. If the company is going to be multigenerational, earnings must be committed to investments that have long-term return, thus reducing the amount available for shareholder dividends. Once a strong foundation has been laid for the business and its growth, a greater percentage of earnings can be allocated in a dividend policy.

Family-owned businesses that want to be multigenerational require a strategic imperative to constantly reinvest. Successful companies generate positive cash flow. The owners of these businesses have several options regarding where to allocate this cash flow. It can be used to support the lifestyle of the owners and their families. It can be optimized to increase EBITDA performance to prepare the business for harvesting.

Multigenerational businesses, however, will strategically reinvest their cash flow to increase capacity and capability by investing in new technologies and in talent management. They are constantly evaluating major new investments. This culture of reinvestment allows the company to respond much more rapidly—and oftentimes opportunistically—to new investment opportunities.

Contrast this reinvestment strategy to that of a company that has been sold to private equity, where upwards of 80 to 90 percent of the free cash flow needs to be committed to paying down the debt undertaken for the overvalued leveraged buyout.

A growing company will face investment choices that look like a kaleidoscope—seductively colorful but somewhat illusive. Consequently, the evaluation of these colorful patterns needs to be made by using a robust strategic planning process that engages the management team. These choices are further evaluated by a competent and qualified independent board of directors.

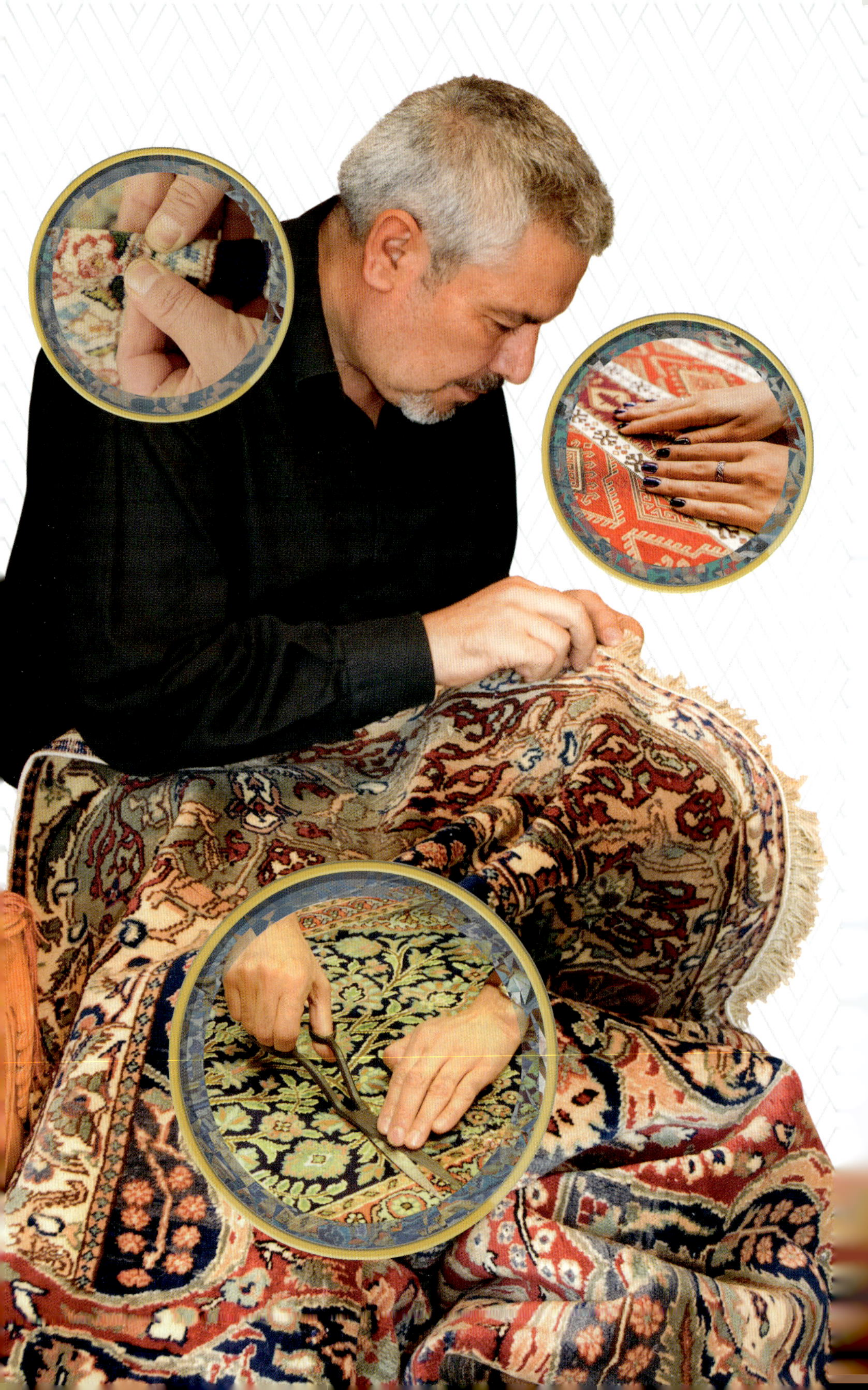

CHAPTER 6

GOVERNANCE

Curating the Tapestry of Heirloom Quality

Following graduation from college, I was elected to the board of directors of Seaman Corporation. The board consisted of my father, our attorney, the manufacturer's rep that was our Vice President of Sales, and me. We met on an annual basis to comply with shareholder regulations. My father would call additional board meetings when he needed approval for major capital investments.

Sound familiar?

This governance model is typical of most privately held growing businesses. It likewise reflects the lack of understanding of the role governance plays in a growing business. Good governance is critical to any business that aspires to sustain multigenerational growth. In fact, a 2014 survey by EY and Kennesaw State University indicates that 90 percent of the largest successful family businesses in the top twenty-one global markets have a board of directors and regularly hold shareholder meetings.[22]

When my father passed away in 1978, my mother replaced him on the board. Her election to the board was to provide her with support as a cofounder of the family business and to confirm the important role she would continue to play.

Soon thereafter, our Vice President of Sales passed away in his mid-fifties. I chose to replace him with another manufacturer's rep who had been a part of our company for nearly twenty years. So, essentially, our new board was simply a replication of the board we had had for the past decade. I had replaced "like for like."

I did try to institute some enhancements to our board governance process, though. I increased the regularity of our meetings to every quarter and added some structure by creating a consistent agenda.

But, I began thinking that board governance could play a more important role in our family business. I considered the board models of public companies. Around this time, I was fortunate to meet Don Noble, CEO and Chairman of Rubbermaid for twenty-one years.

Don took an immediate interest in our family business. Although he was too busy to join our board, he became a "sounding board" for me personally. He also referred me to Leon Danco, a noted family business consultant located in nearby Cleveland.

Leon's career had immersed him in a wide range of family businesses. He became not only a popular family business consultant but also a scholar on the subject, publishing such books as *Inside the Family Business* and *Outside Directors in Family Owned Business*. (His wife was also very involved and authored a book, *From the Other Side of the Bed*, which described the challenges faced by the spouse of the family business founder.)

Both Don and Leon stressed the importance of having an outside board of directors for our company. Because of Don's recommendation and Leon's vast experience with family businesses, I decided to engage this family business guru as a consultant for our family business. Given his "aggressive" consulting fee, this was no small commitment for a family business our size.

Leon had a charming way of describing the characteristics and dynamics of the family business. In conversations with me and, separately, with my family members who resided a distance away in Florida, Leon helped us understand that the business dynamics and tensions present in our family business were not that unique: In fact, they actually represented the norm and are part and parcel of every family business.

Building an Outside Board

Leon's greatest contribution to our family business was convincing my family of the importance of an "outside and independent" board of directors. The timeliness of this advice helped to dispel any notion on the part of my siblings that they might be "entitled" to a seat on the board.

Today, family businesses of all sizes are still burdened by the dominance of family members on the board, adversely impacting the true role that governance should play in a growing business. Research, as noted in *BCG Online*, has affirmed time and again that outside boards are a *fundamental* element of a sustainable, multigenerational company.[23] And yet, I still encounter all kinds of resistance from family business owners to the idea of creating an independent board.

One of the most difficult, yet most critical, understandings of a growing business is distinguishing between the role of shareholders, the role of governance, and the role of management leadership.

In the early stages of a growing business, these roles are most commonly filled by the same people. As a result, shareholder and governance responsibilities are overshadowed by the compelling needs of day-to-day leadership and management. In a growing business, the earlier these role distinctions can be acknowledged and effectively implemented, the stronger the company will become.

Leon Danco helped me understand and define the criteria for outside independent board candidates. These candidates should be experienced business professionals who I might not otherwise be able to solicit for their counsel. Consequently, they should not be professionals who I am already paying for their advice, such as my lawyers or accountants. They certainly should not be anyone on my management team—as I am already paying for their advice and leadership.

I already felt strongly about not considering any of my bankers for my board. If I were facing a financial hurdle, I knew I would ultimately have to discuss it with my banker. First, however, I wanted to get the benefit of counsel from my outside board of directors, and I certainly did not want my banker in the room at that time.

In addition, a banker serving on the board of a customer puts him- or herself in a major conflict of interest. The converse of that conflict is illustrated when I was asked to join the board of a large regional bank. I told the CEO that he could either have my business or have my board service, but not both. I did not want to put myself in a conflict of interest. As noted above, if our company were facing financial hurdles, I would not want my bank to know about them until I had the time to develop a plan of action. If I were on the board of that bank, however, I would have a fiduciary responsibility to disclose those financial hurdles as soon as possible. Hence—no bankers on my board (nor me on theirs!).

At this time, I was a new and active member of the Cleveland Chapter of the Young Presidents Organization. (I had joined three years after my father died.) I asked Leon Danco whether I should consider some of these fellow members as potential Seaman Corporation board candidates. Being familiar with the organization, Leon advised that I could get their input nearly anytime I requested it, so this would not be the best source of board candidates. He reemphasized that I should search for candidates from whom I would not otherwise be able to get advice and counsel.

So began the extended journey of identifying potential board candidates.

Fortunately, I did not feel compelled to quickly increase my four-member board. I was able to take my time identifying candidates and exploring their interest in serving as a board member. The growth of our board was done on an incremental basis.

My personal criteria for board candidates included having a successful business or professional career, bringing needed skills and experience to our board, and expressing a sincere interest in our business and in our family.

Through my networking process, I was able to identify several candidates over the course of time. Some were professionals who had at some point consulted for the business, which had the added benefit of a slight learning curve because they already knew the company.

I would introduce these candidates to my existing board and then to my family shareholders. Sometimes the candidate would be a successful businessman my father and mother knew. In fact, when John Ulman, our attorney on the board, passed away, we replaced him with a confidante of my parents. Over the course of time, our board increased to a total of seven, the majority being independent board members with diverse career backgrounds.

An example of our board included the following:
- a local division manager of Regal Ware, a kitchenware company, with a great deal of manufacturing experience
- a consultant who helped our organization develop our early strategic planning process
- an industrial psychologist we engaged to assess candidates for management positions

I was also very fortunate to have Don Noble graciously serve on our board for several years following his retirement from Rubbermaid in 1980.

At Seaman Corporation, it did not take us long to appreciate the value of an outside board.

Successfully recruiting a board with accomplished directors motivated me to a higher level of leadership performance. If I were to maintain the interest and commitment of these quality resources, our board meetings needed to be dynamic and relevant. Board members would have to feel they were making a contribution and that their input was contributing to the business growth.

As time went on, I added more structure to our business reporting processes. Our financial reporting became more rigorous and was presented in a more meaningful way.

Currently, our board comes together quarterly. We meet in December, around the time of our annual shareholders meeting, and then again in March. In June we go off-site for our meeting. We generally plan the June meeting at a nice venue and encourage the board members to bring their spouses. Fun social activities are planned in addition to corporate business. In August we review our annual plan, which gives our board the opportunity to interact with the management team.

But, it took us some time to develop best practices with our board. As with any new business process, our initial frameworks evolved to accommodate the changing needs of our business.

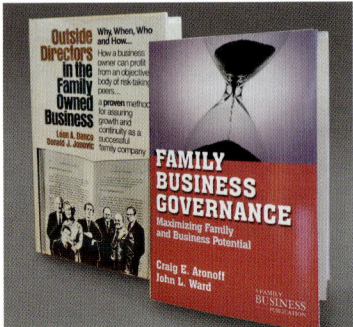

Left: Regular meeting of the Seaman Corporation outside board. Right: Resource books for developing the governance process

If you are just beginning to consider the idea of developing an outside board, two excellent resources for embarking on this journey are Leon Danco and Donald Jonovic's *Outside Directors in the Family Owned Business*[24] and Craig Aronoff and John L. Ward's *Family Business Governance: Maximizing Family and Business Potential*.[25]

The latter is a small handbook, part of the Family Business Consulting Group and Palgrave Macmillan Publishing's Family Business Leadership Series, and focuses especially on managing dynamics between the board and the family, a critical part of the success of utilizing an outside board. While these books were originally published several decades ago, their wisdom remains relevant today.

The Outside Board in a Family Business

If an outside independent board of directors can bring so much value to a growing business, why do most family businesses resist creating an outside board? I have heard many rationalizations.

- "How could anyone know more about my business than I do and provide me with advice?" (Response: Although outside board members may not know as much about the business, they bring different and challenging perspectives that enhance the leadership process by challenging current thinking.)
- "I do not want to commit to the work of managing a board. I have enough to do already." (Response: Managing and engaging an outside board helps the owner step back and "work *on* the business" instead of always "working *in* the business.")
- "An outside board is too expensive. We cannot afford the cost." (Response: An outside board is an investment that offers significant payback.)

And then, of course, there's the unspoken rationale: The owner simply does not want to be vulnerable to the oversight of other people judging his or her leadership performance. I would assert, however, that the owner who has the courage to build an outside board will certainly have that courage well rewarded over time.

Outside Boards as a Resource for the Family

Building an effective outside independent board of directors in the decade following my father's death proved to be critical to the growth and development of our business. Although as President I had a great deal of family shareholder support from my siblings and my mother in the years following my father's death, typical conflicts present in most family businesses began to emerge.

These family business challenges were further aggravated because my mother and siblings lived and worked in Florida for our struggling fabrication division. I lived in Ohio where I managed the business with my leadership team from our company headquarters.

Our outside board played a significant role in helping address these emerging family business issues. When my brothers and sisters became dissatisfied with their career direction in the business, members of the board helped negotiate consulting agreements that allowed them to pursue career directions outside the family business.

Unfortunately, once my siblings left the employ of the family business, it did not resolve their perceived family shareholder issues. Their level of dissatisfaction was further fueled by the local purported family business "consultant" they engaged. This consultant's advice and their subsequent actions illustrated the confusion that often exists in family businesses around the appropriate roles of shareholder, governance, and management leadership.

Were it not for the active and willing participation of our independent board members, these family issues could well have led to the demise of the family business. The board was willing to engage in dialogue with my family regarding their issues. This engagement served as a "buffer" between family shareholders and the management team that continued to run the day-to-day business operations.

Board engagement allowed most of this family discord to occur at the board level and not affect the daily management of the business. As an example, the family business consultant my family hired met primarily with a subcommittee of the board and, therefore, did not engage and distract the leaders at Seaman Corporation.

Our board's involvement with my family became even more critical when my family asked to have their ownership interests purchased by me. Separate negotiations occurred with my siblings' legal counsel, my mother's legal counsel, and, in the background, their business consultant. This process spanned several years. Without the benefit of a highly qualified board, this negotiating process would likely have diverted resources from managing the business and resulted in a negative impact on it.

Countering Entitlement and Motivating Performance

My experience has confirmed the "priceless" role an outside board offers to a family business on many different levels. It is an accessible group of experts with whom you can consult on a regular basis regarding the strategic and tactical direction of your company. It is a group of people whom your family shareholders get to know and respect.

The board helps set the expectations for the role of family shareholders, particularly with respect to governance and management leadership. An active independent board will help buffer that natural "sense of entitlement" that prevails with shareholders of a family business.

An active outside board motivates the CEO/owner to a higher level of performance. Without the rigorous demands of meaningful board meetings and the respect for the accomplished directors, a CEO/owner really has no one to report to. An outside board requires a much higher level of professional performance on the part of the CEO.

To retain engaged and qualified members on your board, the meetings need to be interesting, dynamic, and challenging. This will require that the CEO be involved in leadership challenges that he or she might not otherwise address.

For example, it is one thing to review financial statements monthly and quarterly to satisfy yourself about business results; it is far more challenging to review this financial data and determine how to present these results to an analytical group of outside business experts.

An engaged outside board also impacts the perspectives of your management leadership team. When the management team realizes that the CEO/owner is willing to submit their performance to a qualified and respected group of accomplished businesspeople, they recognize that business decisions are not being made simply at the whim of the owner or family shareholders. They have more faith in business decisions because they understand that these decisions have been evaluated and made on a more objective basis. They will embrace and implement these decisions more effectively.

Oftentimes family businesses fail to have their management leadership engage with the outside board, missing an excellent opportunity to further utilize the value of the board. Making presentations to an accomplished group of business resources will strengthen not only their presentation skills but also their leadership performance. These opportunities also allow the board to evaluate the management team, which is critical to the board's ultimate responsibility for leadership succession.

The outside board likewise plays a critical role in capital investment decisions. A growing multigenerational business will constantly be faced with making significant capital investment decisions. While many of these decisions are made to increase production capacity, many of these decisions are also about increasing capability. Such decisions concern investments in technology platforms that are critical to future growth but may not have short-term payback. An outside board of experienced professionals can add important perspectives to these long-term capital investment decisions.

Countering Entitlement and Clarifying Family Roles in the Business

An engaged, independent board of directors is very important to the long-term sustainability of a growing business. As mentioned earlier, the board can serve as a buffer and diffuse the natural sense of family entitlement. The board can set expectations for shareholders and support the very important concept that owning a family business is a responsibility of stewardship, not entitlement.

An active independent board process will quickly distinguish the role of shareholder, the role of board governance, and the role of management leadership. This process will clarify these three separate and important functions of a sustainable business.

In the absence of an outside board, these roles and responsibilities can become very murky. If the board is comprised primarily of family shareholders, some of whom may also be in management, there is the temptation to tell management what to do and how to do it. And if these family board members have a sense of entitlement, decisions will not be made that support long-term growth and sustainability.

Our board stressed the importance of clarifying the roles of shareholder, director, and manager, particularly when the board was faced with selecting a nonfamily member to succeed me as CEO. We all participated in a facilitated process to better define these roles. The graphics on the following pages reflect the result of this work. Further descriptions are included in Appendix B.

Governance and Leadership

Seaman Corporation

ACTIVE SHAREHOLDERS
Define and communicate ownership expectations. Promote and protect company culture and values. Elect the Board of Directors.

ONGOING COMMUNICATION

IDENTIFY, RECRUIT, (with Chairman and Executive Committee) & ELECT

Reviews, approves, and supports strategy. Oversees the strategic, operational, and financial performance.

BOARD OF DIRECTORS

EXECUTIVE COMMITTEE

CHAIRMAN

Communicate and Collaborate

Consults and collaborates on strategy and key operational issues. Leads the Board oversight of the strategic, operational, and financial performance.

OCCASIONAL COMMUNICATION and SOCIAL INTERACTION

PROVIDE OVERSIGHT

FREQUENT COMMUNICATION   STRATEGIC COLLABORATION

CEO
Leads strategy and operations
Serves as the external face of Seaman Corporation

STRATEGIC LEADERSHIP TEAM
Assists in developing strategy. Responsible for implementing strategy and managing operations.

Major Corporate Decisions Matrix Role Guidelines

	CEO	Non-Executive Chair	Executive Committee	Board[1]	Active Shareholder Group
Shareholder Expectations	ⓘ	<	<	<	✏️👍
Long Range Vision	✏️	<	<	👍	<
Strategic Plan	✏️	<	<	<👍	ⓘ
Business Plan & Budget	✏️	<	<	👍	ⓘ
Capital Expenditures	✏️	<	<	👍	ⓘ👍[2]
Recruits & Hires CEO		<	<	👍	<
CEO Assessment	<ⓘ		✏️	👍	ⓘ
CEO Succession	<	✏️	✏️	👍	ⓘ
Determine CEO Compensation			✏️	👍	ⓘ
Elects Corporate Officers & Approves Compensation	✏️	<	<	👍	ⓘ
Develops Strategic Leadership Team	✏️👍	<	<	ⓘ	ⓘ
Strategic Leadership Team Member Assessment	✏️👍	ⓘ	ⓘ	ⓘ	
Strategic Leadership Team Succession Planning	✏️👍	<	<	<	ⓘ
Elects Board Members	<	✏️	✏️	<	👍[3]
Board Assessment	<	✏️	<	👍	<
New Lines of Business Go/No-Go	✏️👍	<	<	<	
Acquisitions & Divestitures	✏️	<	<	👍	<👍[4]
Change of Control		<	<	👍	👍[3]

✏️ Creates/Proposes   👍 Reviews/Approves   < Contributes/Advises   ⓘ Is Informed

(1) Includes Chairman and Executive Committee   (2) >3-5 Year Payback   (3) All Shareholders   (4) Above Threshold

Board of Directors versus an Advisory Board

I am often asked the question: "Why not create an advisory board instead of a formal board of directors?" Indeed, many closely held businesses have instituted advisory boards in addition to their family-dominated board of directors.

My belief is that having an advisory board is like being "partially pregnant." It lacks a full commitment on the part of the owner and it diminishes much of the value and importance of a legal board.

If you ask someone to serve on an advisory board versus a board of directors, you are minimizing the significance of what you want that person to contribute. If you really want accomplished people to become actively engaged in your business, they will take you far more seriously if the position consists of legal and fiduciary responsibilities rather than simply advisory ones. In addition, family shareholders will respect and take an official legal board far more seriously than a board of directors described as "advisory."

If you question or doubt your ability as a CEO leader, then you might hesitate to create an outside independent board and compromise by establishing an advisory board. A properly empowered board will challenge a CEO—and, quite frankly, should.

Closely held family businesses oftentimes select board members they know will acquiesce to the owner's desires. It is far more demanding to select independent-minded people who will challenge you. To keep these accomplished directors actively engaged, they will not want to feel marginalized. They will want to know that their input is being considered and that they are actually contributing to the growth and development of the business. Board meetings need to be scheduled well in advance for people who otherwise lead very busy lives. Meetings must be managed effectively and efficiently.

As I mentioned earlier in this chapter, our board meets four times a year, and the meetings are always scheduled eighteen months in advance. Information and background for the meetings are sent in advance with adequate time for members to review. When presentations are made by the management team, the focus is on the strategic issues and questions. We have invested in Diligent Board, a software platform used by many Fortune 500 companies and foundations, which allows all this information to be transmitted and reviewed electronically, making each board member's time even more efficient.

Board meetings can be consumed with reviewing ongoing financial performance. Consequently, effective board meetings should quickly focus on the longer-term strategic issues of the business. Board meetings should offer the opportunity to review management's strategic planning process.

Although most board members will not have the time to be actively engaged in the process of strategic planning, this panel of independent and accomplished businesspeople represents an excellent resource to challenge the thinking behind the strategic plan, the assumptions about the external environment, and the strategic direction management has decided to take.

Determining Board Compensation

When considering an outside board, compensation inevitably becomes a topic of conversation. This was one issue where I disagreed with Leon Danco's advice. He suggested that we consider a high level of compensation for the advice a board member will provide.

While the value of their advice is "priceless," I have found that should board candidates be overly concerned about compensation, they are probably not the candidate you want. My first criterion has always been the degree of interest and enthusiasm the candidate has in the business and for the family. If that enthusiasm is there, compensation will become a secondary consideration, and the candidate will likely be a long-term board resource.

That said, a reasonable level of compensation does need to be considered when building an independent board. You can easily benchmark board member compensation by looking at the average for your industry, company size, and the demands on their time. Databases are available that give you guidance for board compensation for private companies. These numbers will vary a great deal.

If you are a small company, do not let the expense deter you from recruiting capable resources. It is important to start the board early. You can always raise board member compensation as your company grows. This was certainly the case with our own board. As our business grew and we better understood who would best serve us, we became better at recruiting the right candidates—and appropriately compensating them.

Succession Planning with the Board

The most significant responsibility of an engaged board of directors is planning for leadership succession. If the business intends to be multigenerational, the board must be sure that competent and qualified leadership is being developed. No owner or CEO is immortal.

In this succession planning process, the board needs to decide if a family member is ready and qualified to succeed as CEO. Or, should the company select a nonfamily member to be CEO? If a nonfamily member is selected to lead the company, that individual will need to develop a strong relationship with family shareholders. An engaged and competent outside board of directors can play a vital role in assuring the development of this shareholder-management relationship.

In the family business conferences I attend, the issue of whether the future CEO should be a family member or a nonfamily member is constantly debated. On one side of the discussion, the argument for a family member to serve in that role is that the culture and legacy of the company is best understood by a family member. A CEO who is a family member will best assure the preservation of these values in the business.

On the other side, the argument is that most of the family's net worth is tied up in and dependent on the success of the business.

The family wants the very best talent to lead the organization and that, in most cases, may well not be a family member. One possible solution to this valid dilemma is for the board to be committed to selecting the very best person for the CEO leadership role—family or nonfamily—and have a qualified family member always serve as the Chairman of the Board.

Succession planning in a successful privately held family business is much more complex and challenging than managing the business itself. The success of the business most often reflects the talent, skills, personality, and intuitive sense of the CEO/owner. The culture of the company is a reflection of the traits of the longtime CEO. The shareholders, the board, and the CEO him- or herself must recognize that this personality and these unique characteristics will not be easily, if at all, replaceable. Therefore, leadership development for succession is a multiyear process. And the very structure of the organization may be affected by this succession planning process.

In the case of our family business, where I served as CEO for nearly forty years, this reality occurred when my COO of fifteen years, and my contemporary, went to my board and announced he planned to retire in two years.

Once the board fully understood his day-to-day responsibilities, they became more concerned about COO succession planning, which was imminent, than they were about CEO succession. They also understood that the COO leadership development and succession process would significantly influence the ultimate succession process for the CEO.

Working with the leadership committee of the board, we created a leadership development program prior to selecting internal candidates for this process. It consisted of the multi-week management development program at the Harvard Business School, the engagement of a leadership coach, and, ultimately, inclusion in the CEO-COO business retreats I held on a quarterly basis.

Once this leadership development program was created, and with the input from board members, we selected two internal candidates for this two-year course. As the process evolved, and with the counsel and support of the leadership coach, we focused on a coleadership model. The two candidates became Executive Vice Presidents, followed by promotion to Co-Presidents to replace the COO position. The board actively considered the possibility of Co-CEOs, which would certainly affect the leadership structure of the organization.

During this process, the active engagement of these two candidates with our outside board became an extremely valuable part of their leadership development. Subsequently, the involvement of the board proved to be invaluable to the succession process itself. While we observed that both candidates brought unique skills to their leadership roles, their close and trusted working relationship created an effective and unique leadership model for the business.

Through their continual engagement with our board, however, it became evident that the leadership growth in one of the candidates was more rapid than in the other. Perhaps even more critical, that candidate had a leadership style that was more consistent with the culture of the company. As a result, he was promoted to COO. The other very competent coleader was transitioned out to a larger organization, where he became a division president and subsequently selected as the CEO for a private-equity-owned company.

Our board's next task was to help facilitate the succession of this newly trained COO to becoming the first nonfamily CEO of Seaman Corporation, replacing a family member who had served as CEO for forty years. This process included enhancing the roles and fiduciary responsibilities of the board itself.

It also required further clarifying the role of family shareholders, their financial and nonfinancial performance expectations for the family business, the role of the outside board of directors, and the role and responsibilities of management leadership. The result of this work is detailed in Appendix B (mentioned previously). Over the next two years, this leadership succession was successfully transitioned.

A unique and important component of a multigenerational family business strategy is developing the governance process early. An independent outside board will drive the CEO to a higher standard of leadership. Regular, well-managed board meetings will challenge the thinking of the CEO and the management team.

Unfortunately, most family businesses fail to see the value of an outside board and do not spend the time necessary to develop this governance process for any number of reasons. They do not understand the very purpose and value an outside board can bring to the growth and development of a business.

Citing once more the 2014 survey by EY and Kennesaw State University, as of 2014, 90 percent of successful multigenerational family businesses worldwide commit to an outside board.[26] The influence of these boards of directors on the multigenerational success of a family business cannot be underrated.

A multigenerational growing business is faced with a kaleidoscope of colorful patterns from which to choose. Management leadership is responsible for strategically selecting design patterns they can then weave into a beautiful tapestry.

While a board of directors is not responsible for selecting and weaving these colorful patterns, a governance process comprised of an engaged independent outside board can be the curator of the beauty and the longevity of this wonderful tapestry called a family business.

"Preserving Family Values"

CHAPTER 7

SHAREHOLDER EDUCATION AND ENGAGEMENT

Stewarding the Tapestry through Generations

Shirtsleeves to shirtsleeves—in three generations.
Clogs to clogs—in three generations.
Rice paddy to rice paddy—in three generations.
Stall to stall—in three generations.

—Unknown

The universality of this proverb across ages and cultures makes it a description of human nature itself. In particular, these words are most often spoken today to describe the journey of a family business. The founder rolls up his shirtsleeves and, with a great deal of sweat equity, creates the foundation for a family business.

The second generation continues to run the business but retains the memories of the hard work and effort, the sacrifices and the values that were so much a part of the parents' success. But their lifestyle continues to improve and they bestow the fruits of wealth on their children, mostly funded by the free cash flow of the business.

The third generation, now with ever-more family shareholders, feels entitled to what they perceive to be unlimited wealth created by the founding grandparents. They are so far removed from the founder's work experience that they do not appreciate the work ethic, the culture, and the values that were required to create the family business. Alternatively, the second generation does not adequately trust or prepare the following generations for stewardship and are unwilling to "give up the reins" in time to manage a successful transition.

Management leadership passes from one family member to another, with little consideration of qualifications or capabilities. A larger number of family shareholders continue to extract value from the business. It does not take long for this family business to confront its demise.

Hence, by the time the fourth generation arrives, they now need to roll up their sleeves and begin working again.

This scenario in one form or another plays itself out time and time again, particularly in *American family businesses*. In this country's family business culture, a sense of entitlement predominates rather than a responsibility of stewardship. Family businesses are oftentimes used as ATM machines to support the family's lifestyles. Or they are managed with the intent of harvesting through a future liquidity event. There is the paradigm that if you grow up in a family business, you are entitled to its output and benefits.

Parents perpetuate this culture when they address succession planning. The children who commit to working in the family business are given ownership shares. Those who do not work in the family business are compensated with "comparable value," perpetuating the concept of birthright and entitlement.

In actuality, family businesses are a special treasure. Family businesses create new jobs for our society. Family businesses instill and maintain unique cultural values. Family businesses are often the philanthropic leaders in their communities, providing both money and time (as volunteers). As I mentioned in the introduction, according to the 2017 Edelman Trust Barometer Survey, family businesses enjoy a double-digit trust advantage over businesses in general.[27] More than twice as many respondents replied that they would prefer to work for a family business. And 45 percent of the respondents said they would be willing to pay more if they knew they were buying from a family business. Family business ownership is a responsibility of stewardship, not a birthright or an entitlement.

Family businesses are responsible for the livelihood of all the employees and their families. When the business is used to support personal lifestyles or when the business is "harvested" through a liquidity event, these employee family livelihoods are put at risk.

If you are fortunate enough to be born into a family business, do not think of it as a birthright or an entitlement. You have been chosen to be the steward of an economic enterprise that provides the livelihood for many other families and contributes to the vitality of the community.

The Case for Shareholder Education

Because of our cultural norms and because it is human nature to be possessive, it is easy to understand why the descendants of the founder of a family business feel a sense of birthright or entitlement. Consequently, if a company is going to be multigenerational, family shareholder education is vital.

Keeping the history of the family business alive by teaching future generations the sacrifices, the values, and the culture of the founder's generation will instill principles of stewardship. As young family shareholders are growing up, it is important for them to learn the value of the work ethic, the economics of making a living, and the responsibility of stewardship.

While these principles are important to everyone in our society, family businesses offer a unique opportunity to instill these values in generations of our young people. It is important that we take advantage of this opportunity, particularly if we want to create a multigenerational family business.

One phenomenon I have observed that can result from not having a family shareholder education process is that future generations easily take for granted the hard work and effort required to build, to grow, and to sustain a business in an ever-changing economy. In some cases, the future generations see the family business as an entitlement and continue to extract value away from the business. In other cases, future generations fail to recognize the challenges of creating wealth and they support policies that try to redistribute this wealth.

While this redistribution may be well intended, in so many cases it simply "kills the goose that lays the golden egg." As author Leslie Dashew puts it, "Sustainable development means meeting the needs of the present without compromising the ability of future generations to meet their own needs."[28]

In other words, create a "gaggle of geese" that keep on producing eggs for the future.

A paradigm in today's family business culture is that responsibility and stewardship rest solely with those family members who want to pursue their career in the business. Early shareholder education will explain how there are many ways to steward the ownership of a family business without having to commit to a career in the business. This education will set the expectations for "active shareholder" involvement and allow family members to pursue careers outside the family business.

Early shareholder education will help clarify the opportunities for careers in the family business and may well motivate next-generation family shareholders to pursue those careers or transition back to the family business after career experience elsewhere. This education process is an investment in future family leadership which will help sustain a multigenerational business.

The Challenges of Shareholder Education

Instilling the values of a business founder becomes more challenging when future generations become further removed from those early start-up years. So, it becomes even more important to invest in family shareholder education. And the best place to begin is by sharing the history of the company in an accurate and comprehensive manner that includes the principles and values of the founders.

Proactive shareholder education became a challenge following my father's death in 1978 at the premature age of fifty-five. As I described in the previous chapter, my mother and two brothers and two sisters continued to live in Florida and work in our financially struggling division. One thousand miles separated their day-to-day lives and careers from my day-to-day life in Ohio where our management team resided.

I attempted to bridge this gap by focusing on our governance process. I committed to quarterly board meetings. Once a year, I scheduled a three-day off-site board meeting that included all family shareholders, including the grandchildren.

These meetings were held in such attractive locations as Captiva Island in Florida and Hilton Head in Georgia. The agenda consisted of business and financial presentations to the board and the family shareholders. We also incorporated a number of family and board social activities.

After several years of these events, my mother and my siblings recommended that we discontinue them. They felt that the expense was too great and they did not see the value. Because they were located a thousand miles from the management team and they were working in a struggling division, it was understandable that they perceived these shareholder and board events as an unnecessary expense.

Unfortunately, this decision removed the primary venue in which to develop an effective shareholder education process. Shortly thereafter, our problematic family business issues arose.

We experienced family divergence between the way my management team and I were running the business and the way my Florida family thought the business should be run. The Florida family shareholders were updated quarterly on the company's financial performance. Nonetheless, they felt a need to have more input into the day-to-day operations.

As an example, our board members received a letter signed by my mother (who sat on the board) and my siblings requiring monthly financial reports and inclusion in the management decision-making process.

From my perspective, their perception seemed to be: "This is the business our father left us and we are entitled to run it and receive its benefits." This sense of entitlement to the business created by our father ultimately extended down to the grandchildren. Many of them felt entitled to the family business benefits they perceived were left directly to them by their grandfather, irrespective of what the financial performance of the company was at the time of his death.

While the foundation of the family business created by the founder and his wife had significant value, there was not an understanding of the work and effort required to both sustain and grow the business for a much larger group of family shareholders.

This sense of entitlement drives behavior that can be destructive to a family business. By contrast, a sense of responsibility for stewardship drives a different set of behaviors that are much more positive.

An effective shareholder education process creates an understanding of this stewardship role and a set of expectations of ownership. It communicates the privilege of being a part of this unique treasure. It establishes a positive set of behaviors and expectations for the next generation of family shareholders.

Unfortunately, for a variety of very understandable reasons, my family did not get the opportunity to explore, adopt, and instill these principles of stewardship into our family business process. Instead, we went down the path that many, if not most, family businesses travel. My mother and siblings' family business consultant was quick to validate their perceptions of what was wrong with our family business and the way our management team and I were leading it.

Over the course of several years, my family and their adviser held many meetings with me and many of our board members trying to understand and resolve their issues. Ultimately, my mother and my siblings requested that I purchase their interests in our family business entities. More than a year later, we successfully negotiated an agreement that provided them with a generous payout and I became the primary owner.

An Evolving Model of Shareholder Participation

Following the buyout, planning for succession became a totally different strategic issue. Instead of five siblings and ten grandchildren, succession planning now involved only my wife, Judy, me, and our three children.

After the 1994 buyout, I spent many years thinking about succession planning and the future of our family business. The family turmoil and disruption with my mother and my siblings during this time period distanced my children from their grandmother, aunts and uncles, and cousins. There was little desire on their part to become involved in the family business.

At a business conference, I had the opportunity to reconnect with John Ward, a family business consultant I had met twenty years prior. His presentation focused on the research he conducted over the course of twenty years, studying 5,000 family businesses specifically to understand multigenerational succession.

His research, detailed in his book *Perpetuating the Family Business*, revealed that less than 5 percent of family businesses were successfully passed beyond the third generation.[29]

John's research went further to focus on the small percentage of family businesses that were successful. Were there unique traits or processes that helped those businesses maintain success over multiple generations?

From this research, John developed the concept of "active shareholder" as a family business ownership model. This ownership model did not require the next generation to commit their careers to the family business. These family members did, however, want to see the founder's legacy carried forward. They wanted to preserve the values and culture created by the founder while giving management leadership the freedom to manage the business for survival and growth in the ever-changing economic environment.

After understanding this model of family business ownership, I thought it might appeal to our children, who at this point had no interest in a career in the family business. This became my motivation for beginning our shareholder education process. I wanted to expose our children to this ownership model without them feeling compelled to commit to it.

We were fortunate that John was available to work with my family and my board for the beginning of this education process.

Over a short period of time, my family was attracted to the potential of this family business ownership model. It was the beginning of seeing the family business as a stewardship responsibility and a way in which active ownership might be integrated into their lives.

As an example, our second daughter spent a year abroad working in Chile. Upon her return, she asked me if she could spend a year or so learning about the family business by working in it. Four years later, she was still working for the family business and only left to gain additional work experience in New York City. A decade later she and her family decided to move back to Wooster, Ohio, partly because she felt at least one of the future owners of the family business should reside in the Wooster community.

The Family Mission Statement and Handbook

Working with John Ward and his staff, my family made early progress in better understanding the value and importance of active shareholder ownership. All three of our children actively participated in this process. We worked together to create formal guidelines and a set of family business policies, such as guidelines for family employment.

John helped us address the important policies involved with active shareholders. It did not take us long to realize that we were embarking on a journey that few family businesses took.

As an example, when John began working with our company, he was surprised and impressed that we had an engaged outside board of directors. Among the vast majority of his consulting clients, he had to assist them in creating this model, which is essential to successful active ownership.

As we continued to explore the purposes for investing our time in active ownership of the family business, our children began to embrace the concept of stewardship. They quickly began to understand and appreciate that the livelihoods of our many associates depended on the success of the family business.

The Mission Statement

One interesting task in this family education process was to create a family mission statement. We all worked together on this process. While we had a business mission statement that had been created years before, my children were insistent that we not try to incorporate the business mission statement into our family mission.

Once we agreed on the principles of our family mission statement, they then took a look at the business mission statement and were pleasantly surprised to see how much alignment there was between the two documents.

The Seaman Family Mission Statement

Our Mission is to realize our potential as a family by recognizing each person as an individual, possessing unique talents from which each of us can learn.

We will

> *practice good health, creativity, innovation, initiative, and acceptance of responsibility*
>
> *permit each other's growth in the pursuit of personal, spiritual and career aspirations*
>
> *be adventurous and courageous, expanding our cultural breadth and knowledge by traveling in body, mind, and spirit to new destinations*
>
> *participate in our communities, serving as responsible citizens, and lending our hands to those less fortunate*
>
> *Appreciate the journey of each day and enjoy the blessings and opportunities it provides*
>
> *Preserve home as a safe place where we can love and enjoy the company of each other*

Our true stewardship is the commitment of these values to future generations

July, 1998

Each of our children was impacted by this education process in a different way. Our son was in his teenage years when we started shareholder education. Consequently, his involvement can be described as a bit more passive, but he nonetheless learned a great deal by being present.

When he started to get serious about a long-term career direction, he asked his mother and me if he could begin with a job in the business. He said he did not want to pursue another career and ten years down the road wonder whether or not he should have tried the family business. If he had a few years of work experience in the business and then pursued a different career, he would not have to question that decision.

A Family Business Manual

Once Judy and I realized the opportunity we had to create a multigenerational family business, we also recognized the amount of time investment that needed to be made and we did not hesitate to make this commitment. We knew that success would be very dependent on the education of future shareholders. Our oldest daughter agreed to lead this responsibility and we committed to the investment in consultants to assist her.

We focused on creating a number of basic policies that then evolved into a family business manual. Simply reading the contents of this manual gives insight into the complexity of owning a family business, well beyond the day-to-day business operations.

The family business manual becomes an important tool for the education of future shareholders. It helps present the expectations of shareholder involvement and how the business will operate. It will support the principle of stewardship that comes with family business ownership.

As the business grows and as the family grows, the family business manual should be reviewed on a regular basis to keep it relevant. As an example, we reviewed our policy manual to determine if any policies needed to be changed or modified once we elected a nonfamily CEO.

A VIBRANT VISION

The Seaman Family Governance Handbook. The Table of Contents lists the many components of the family governance process.

With the current success of our business and a growing asset base, our family may be investing in several value-creating businesses in the future. So, we are in the process of evolving from being primarily a family operating business to becoming a family enterprise that may hold a number of value-creating assets, including a family investment fund. In addition, the family will have involvement in the philanthropic foundation Judy and I created many years ago. We also recognize the significance of the growing number of next-generation family shareholders.

Our family business manual is now evolving into a family constitution. Once again, reviewing the components of a family constitution that were developed by the Family Business Consulting Group and are presented on the following page illustrates the impressive complexity of a multigenerational family business

Common Elements of Family Constitutions

Purpose	Shareholders' Meeting
Purpose of the Family Constitution	Next Generation Development
Family Guiding Principles/Core Values	Policies & Statements
	Definition of Family
Family Mission Statement	Eligibility for Ownership
Family Objectives	Family Employment
Structures/Entities	Family Compensation
Purpose, structure, representation, oversight, policies and so on relating to:	Family Performance Management/ Termination
	Retirement from the Enterprise
Family Council	Responsibilities, Roles & Rights of Shareholder
Family Office	
Family Foundation	Ownership Transfer
Committees/Task Forces	Stock Valuation
Business/Operating Company	Dividends and Reserves
Family Vision for the Company	Conflict of Interest
Strategic Planning Process	Code of Conduct
Guidance on Growth, Risk, Profitability, and Liquidity	Meeting Ground Rules
	Conflict Resolution
Purpose of the Board of Directors	Confidentiality
Procedures	Media/Public relations
Nominations/Elections	Family Benefits
Meetings	Education
Decision Making	Housing
Communications	Medical/Dental
Expenses & Budgeting	Insurance
Buying & Selling Family Assets	Automobiles
Funding Entrepreneurial Ventures	Retirement
Keeping/Maintaining Family History	Vacation
	Travel
Amending the Constitution	

Copyright © 2017 The Family Business Consulting Group, Inc. All rights reserved.

Early Shareholder Education and Preserving Cultural History

It is never too early to start shareholder education. In the case of my children, I was hesitant to expose them to the family business at an early age because of the challenging issues that existed with my mother and siblings. It would also have been difficult to have all the grandchildren receive the same exposure because of the geographic separation.

So, my children did not get exposed to the concept of family business as a treasure or the responsibility of stewardship until they were in their late teens and early twenties. It was only after we discovered and began to understand John Ward's research on active shareholders that we began the process of shareholder education. It would take some years to institutionalize this process into the culture of our family business.

Creating a culture of stewardship can first be accomplished by teaching the history of the family business. This is the opportunity to showcase the work ethic of the founders, the blood, sweat, and tears, the challenges, and the sacrifices that were made to start and build the foundation of the family business.

Many lessons and values can be taught by sharing the history of the family business and telling how it started and what challenges it faced. Principles of entrepreneurship, integrity, and social responsibility are oftentimes a significant part of the growth of a family business.

Because I recognized the value of preserving the history of our family business, I engaged an author to research and write a history of our company as part of celebrating our fifty years in business in 1999. This book is entitled *The First 50 Years* and presents the early struggles of creating an industrial fabric business along with many stories that capture the historic lore of the family business. In 2009, I asked the author to update our history. We had experienced such a dynamic decade that the book actually doubled in size and today stands as an excellent tome about the growth and development of a successful family business.

A History of the Seaman Corporation
1949—2009

Shareholder education will instill a sense of responsibility in the employees who helped the founder start and grow the business. These employees and the livelihood of their families depend on the continuing success of the family business. So, while there is financial and personal growth value in being involved with the family business, there is also a significant stewardship responsibility.

I observed the importance of preserving the cultural history of a business with two large and well-respected Fortune 500 companies in our own community, Rubbermaid and Smuckers. It is nearly impossible to find a written history of the founding, growth, and development of Rubbermaid. By contrast, the history and cultural values of Smuckers is omnipresent and celebrated, even embedded in their commercials and packaging.

I watched the virtual demise of Rubbermaid, one of Fortune 500's most admired companies, as its leadership focused primarily on financial results for its shareholders and ultimately sold to Newell, where only its brand name barely survives today. By contrast, Smuckers has institutionalized its history and culture and kept these values a priority while continuing to achieve financial performance. Today the company is many times the size Rubbermaid was when it was purchased by Newell.

We are being much more proactive with our own grandchildren now. We are creating family business blocks of education—that is, picture books and a formalized curriculum—which include relevant subjects such as:

- What is money
- What is currency
- What is profit and loss
- What are the principles of entrepreneurship
- What is the history of Seaman Corporation
- What is philanthropy

By staying focused on the history of the company and the values of the founder, we can connect our values-based principles to the family business. With this foundation in place, our grandchildren will have a solid understanding of the family business when they begin making decisions about their careers. If they choose careers outside the family business, the principles they are learning will continue to serve them well. They will see opportunities to stay engaged with the family business as an active shareholder. One of the blessings of a family business is having the opportunity to teach these principles to the next generation, regardless of their career choices.

We try to integrate shareholder education with family gatherings, but we are careful to separate the business education components from family togetherness activities. In fact, we are very deliberate about having family gatherings with no mention of family business.

An example of integrating shareholder education was at one of our recent off-site multiday board meetings where the entire family, including grandchildren, attended. During a business session, the activity planned for the grandchildren was a craft project where they were asked to create products utilizing the fabrics produced by the family business. After they completed their individual projects, they were given the opportunity to present their crafts to the board of directors.

Another recent example of our family shareholder education process was an event scheduled at our Bristol, Tennessee, manufacturing facility. All our children and grandchildren, ages one to sixteen, participated. We showcased our weaving and coating capabilities, which the grandchildren found very fascinating. We then enjoyed a special Tennessee barbeque luncheon with all our associates.

This was an opportunity to illustrate the large number of associates and their families that are dependent on the continuing success of our business. In addition, there was great benefit in our associates seeing that we were engaging future generations in the understanding our family business.

A very important message is sent to company associates when they see active shareholder education. People who work for a family business are always concerned about what will happen to the business when the CEO retires or might have an untimely serious health problem. There is ample evidence that subsequent events could have adverse consequences on their jobs and livelihood.

In addition, customers can become concerned and resist becoming dependent on a supplier with no succession plan. But when associates and customers see future generations being educated in the business in a thoughtful way, they have much more confidence in the future of the company.

Visible shareholder education also helps in recruiting strong talent for the board of directors or for management leadership. Educating future shareholders helps to diffuse the anxious feelings that are normal when working for a family business.

Good shareholder education combined with an engaged outside board gives leadership talent the confidence that the business is not being influenced solely by the idiosyncrasies of the owner. They will feel a greater sense of empowerment and feel that their leadership will influence the future direction of the company. Their ideas will be reviewed by not only the CEO/owner but also by a quality board of directors and by an informed group of family shareholders.

One of the goals of a shareholder education program is to instill the concept that owning and successfully growing a family business for future generations is a "call to a greater cause." Most entrepreneurial start-ups today are motivated by creating a business that will ultimately have a liquidation event. Too often this creates financial wealth for the founder/owners but does little for the employees who helped achieve the results. It is a much greater challenge to create a business with the strategic objective to make it multigenerational.

Contrast the choice of building a business and harvesting it through a liquidation event. The owner will benefit from the funds received and, in all likelihood, will allocate some of the funds to a philanthropic cause. The jobs of the employees, however, will in many cases remain at risk. If, on the other hand, the created business successfully grows and is handed down to future generations, the business will continue to provide jobs and generate funding continuously.

Teaching philanthropy and how it is funded is an essential part of family shareholder education. Once established, family businesses are capable of allocating a portion of their earnings for social responsibility, often through a family or community foundation.

Nevertheless, when teaching this philanthropic value, it is important to stress that the funding for these foundations and subsequent grants could not and will not continue to exist without a well-run business that achieves positive financial performance. The funds available for a philanthropic foundation are only achieved through the hardworking effort of the employees of the family business.

Resources for Building Shareholder Education

An effective process for shareholder education consists of many components and can appear to be overwhelming. Fortunately, there are resources from a wide variety of family business organizations that can provide guidelines and support for this process.

The "Pyramid of Family Ownership" created by Amy Shuman of the Family Business Consulting Group is a good representation of how to build continuity for family business success. The foundation of her pyramid is built on the guiding principles and aspirations that reflect the purpose, values, and vision of the family business.

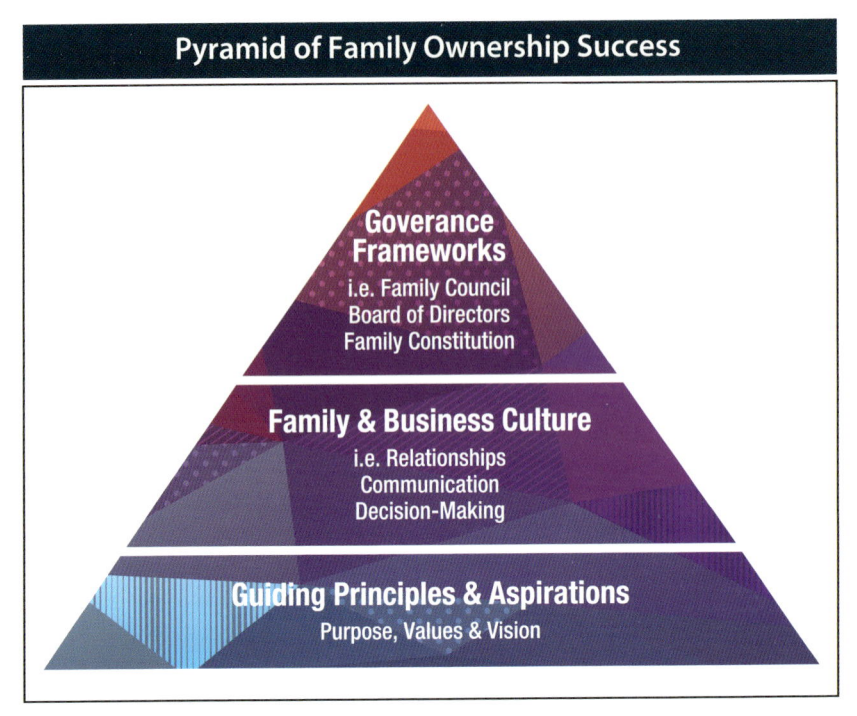

Pyramid of Family Ownership Success

Goverance Frameworks
i.e. Family Council
Board of Directors
Family Constitution

Family & Business Culture
i.e. Relationships
Communication
Decision-Making

Guiding Principles & Aspirations
Purpose, Values & Vision

(Note: pyramid created by Amy Schuman, principal consultant with The Family Business Consulting Group, Inc)

Family businesses are always faced with the challenge of next-generation shareholders perceiving their inherited ownership as one of entitlement instead of stewardship. Early shareholder education will help "-nip this sense of entitlement in the bud-" and thus hopefully prevent the "shirtsleeves to shirtsleeves in three generations" experience.

While combating entitlement is a significant objective of shareholder education, this process can also help future family shareholders decide what, if any, role they want to play in family business ownership. Stewardship requires an investment in both time and effort, and future generations will have many competing choices. The purpose of a quality shareholder education process is to help future generations make better informed decisions around the opportunities and challenges of a family business and the other life choices they will certainly have.

Shareholder education must include keeping future generations aware of the strategic challenges facing the family business enterprise. Too often, financial performance of successful family businesses is taken for granted. Being disconnected from the reality of these business challenges will cause future family shareholders to focus more on the allocation of cash flow—via dividends or distributions—to their trusts to support their lifestyles.

A primary priority of shareholder stewardship is to assure that the board of directors selects management leadership capable of addressing the ever-changing strategic challenges of the family business enterprises. If the shareholders are not kept aware of these strategic challenges, they will not be able to hold their board accountable for this important responsibility.

A kaleidoscope of chaotic and colorful choices will always be faced by shareholders of family businesses. Engagement by family shareholders can make these choices even more chaotic and colorful.

With a proactive quality shareholder education process, though, engaged family shareholders can play a very important role in the design and quality of the tapestry that is created by the company's weavers. And shareholder education is vital to the heirloom quality of this tapestry, a tapestry that is multigenerational and sustainable.

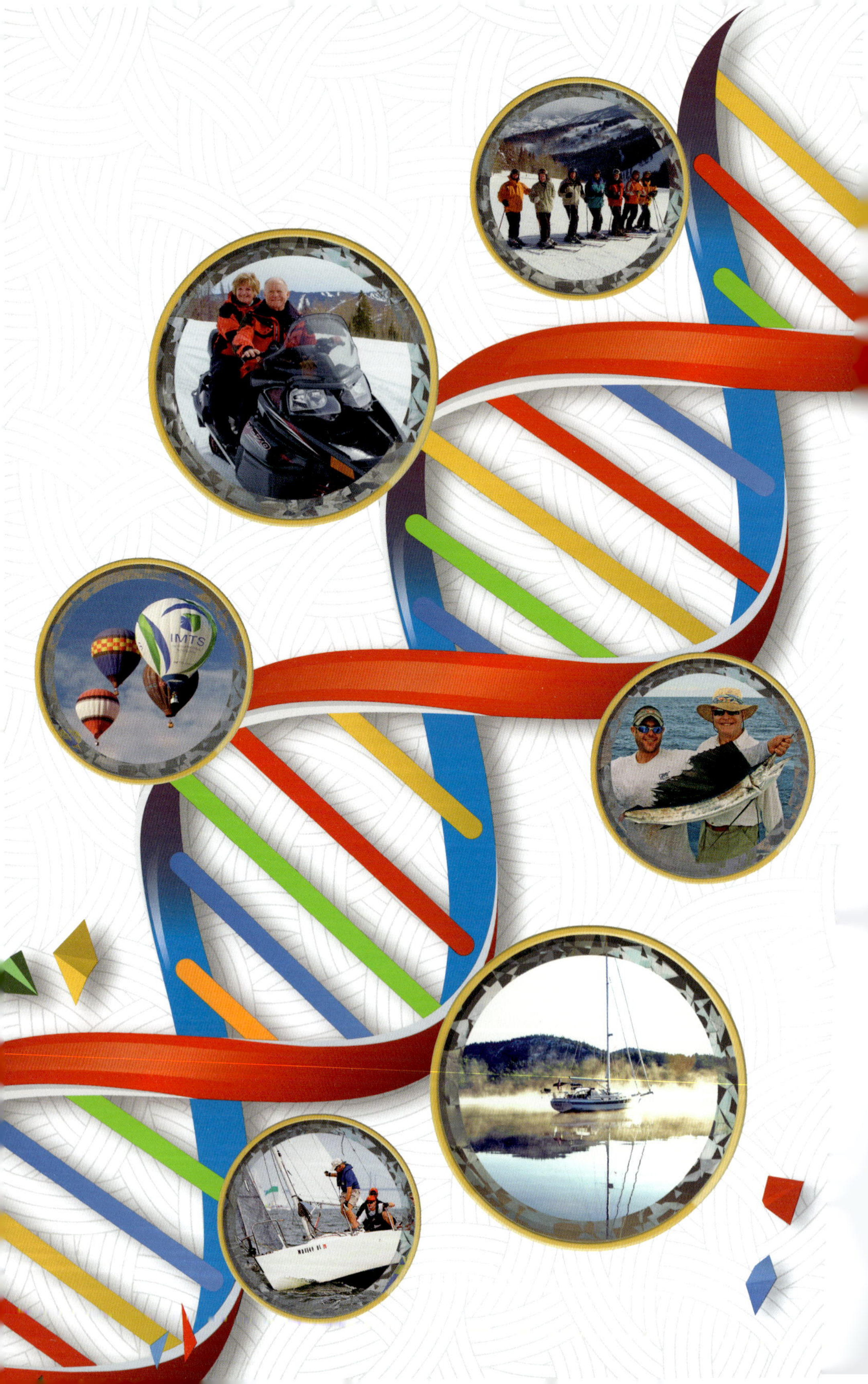
IMTS

CHAPTER 8

SUSTAINING YOURSELF THROUGH THE JOURNEY

Nourishing Your Enduring Spirit

*Entrepreneurship is the **joy** of creating a vision,*
*The **discipline** of developing a strategy,*
*And the **passion** for executing the journey.*

— Richard Seaman

Life is a kaleidoscope of choices: family, career, travel, education, hobbies, and other personal passions—even those after-work choices of TV entertainment among the hundreds of cable channels and a myriad of streaming services.

If you own your own business, this kaleidoscope can become very one-dimensional as you allow your "passion for executing the journey" to consume most of your twenty-four-hour day. How do you keep your kaleidoscope of life balanced, colorful, and multidimensional?

In 1962, my father hired my uncle to be the production supervisor for our small manufacturing business. My uncle moved his wife and four young daughters to our Millersburg, Ohio, community. Two years later, he was diagnosed with cancer and passed away in his late forties.

Early one June morning in 1970, I received a call from a very good friend of my wife's family. He regretfully informed me that my father-in-law passed away of a heart attack on a flight from Columbus to Los Angeles the evening before. He was fifty-two.

In 1976 my father was diagnosed with lung cancer. After a courageous battle, he passed away. He was fifty-five.

Within two years of my father's passing, our national sales manager died of heart failure. He was fifty-four.

Also within two years of my father's passing, the partner in our CPA firm who served as our financial adviser passed away of cancer. He was in his late fifties.

Within one year after our attorney, the secretary of the company, retired at the age of sixty-five, he too was diagnosed with cancer and passed away shortly thereafter.

I was in my twenties and early thirties when these important men in my life and in our business experienced a premature end to their life's journey and all its aspirations. These tragic events certainly played a significant role in my emerging philosophy of life.

These early and premature deaths refuted the paradigm work hard until you retire in your mid-sixties and then enjoy the passions of your life. I became acutely aware of the value of personal health and recognized that there is no assurance that our own life's journey will continue for another year, another month, or even another twenty-four hours. While I always look to the future with an optimistic eye, I never presume that I will actually be a participant in that future.

Although building and managing a growing family business consumed a great deal of my time and attention, I consistently tried to balance this commitment with the important and significant relationships and experiences that I wanted to create in my kaleidoscope of life.

The singular dimension of my parents' lives also influenced my day-to-day choices. My mother and father worked extremely hard in starting and creating our family business while at the same time raising five children on our forty-two-acre farm in Millersburg, Ohio. My father was involved in the lives of the family, but his mind was nearly 24/7 on the opportunities and challenges of our growing business.

His only escape from this entrepreneurial passion occurred during our summer boating weekends on Lake Erie or when he was searching for a boat or aircraft upgrade. Fortunately, this occurred every two to three years. My father and mother always dreamed of a future that would include extensive cruising and traveling.

Unfortunately, this future disappeared when my father passed away. Neither he nor my mother would ever regret their life's choices or their commitment to create a family business; however, their quality of life balance was, by necessity, narrowly defined.

During these years of growing up in the family business, I also observed the peers of my parents. In so many cases, the father's focus on his career was to the detriment of his relationship with his children; oftentimes he was even estranged from them.

Early in my career, I recognized that I had a rare and unique opportunity—the chance to build and grow a successful business. My father and mother had already built a good foundation for this family business.

Because of the many events and experiences described above, I decided that if I were the most successful businessman in the country, but that success came at the expense of my health, of my marriage, and of my family relationships, or if my children did not grow up to be responsible and accountable, then I would consider myself a failure in life, regardless of the financial success of our family business. I also recognized that the family business model of my parents would not work well with my family.

Quality of Life Balance

Consequently, I decided early in my career to balance my work-life schedule by including a fun factor in my business commitments.

For example, when I recognized that my leadership responsibilities in the family business were going to require travel away from home, I consciously decided to make these trips enjoyable.

I searched out opportunities to meet with friends located in my travel areas. I looked for restaurants where I could share an enjoyable meal with my friends, my customers, my suppliers, or simply a quiet evening by myself. I availed myself of opportunities to enjoy the uniqueness of the areas where I traveled.

If a convention or business meeting was near water, I would charter a boat on which to entertain customers and business associates. Enjoying the passion for growing my business did not have to be at the exclusion of enjoying the other passions in my life.

As I mentioned before, another example of the value of balancing work and pleasure were the CEO-COO retreats that I planned after I introduced the role of Chief Operating Officer to the company. I committed to having off-site retreats once a quarter to achieve strategic and tactical alignment between my COO and myself. We held these retreats religiously for more than fifteen years.

During a CEO-COO retreat, Richard Seaman and John Crum, his COO, enjoy a Segway tour of Washington, DC.

Each retreat involved a full and intense meeting agenda. I selected locations that were enjoyable venues, such as ski and golf resorts, and other locations that offered a variety of recreational activities, such as fishing and sailboat charters. On one retreat, we enjoyed a Segway tour of Washington, DC.

Our days included dinners at fine restaurants. Incorporating recreational and social activities into our agenda of challenging topics resulted in more productive discussions and made these days away from home more enjoyable. Such commitments were incrementally costlier in terms of both money and time, but the investment produced priceless results, particularly in the bond of trust and alignment that developed between me and my COO.

One of the great values of owning and operating your own business is the relative freedom you have to manage your own schedule. Of course, that is somewhat dictated by the day-to-day demands of the business, but compared to working for another company, public or private, self-employment offers a great deal more freedom—or at least more influence—regarding your scheduling decisions.

So, if you have the privilege of making the decisions on how you spend your time, take advantage of using that freedom to create your own colorful kaleidoscope.

Invest in Your Hobbies

I wanted my kaleidoscope of life to be as multidimensional and colorful as possible. I intentionally chose to allocate time to those activities for which I developed an early passion. This investment became a high priority if these activities or hobbies enhanced my family relationships or my relationships with friends.

When I became fascinated with photography, I took several weekend courses to understand and develop my photographic skills. Judy and I took skiing lessons early in our marriage. Our enjoyment of the sport developed into a lifelong recreational activity for our family, our children, and now our grandchildren. I also used skiing opportunities to develop and strengthen customer relationships.

My fascination with photography evolved in an unexpected way. Shortly before my father-in-law passed away, he made a business trip to Japan. Having a modest interest in photography himself, he purchased a Minolta SLR camera.

Following his death, my mother-in-law passed this nearly new camera down to me. I actually owned the camera for more than two years before I realized the lens could be removed and was interchangeable with other lenses. Attending weekend seminars enhanced my photographic imagination and creative skills.

While I have continued to pursue my interest in photography, participating in its evolution through the digital revolution and mirrorless cameras, the basic essence of this hobby for me has remained the same. Trying to capture the activities and stages of my children and grandchildren has enhanced my engagement with their lives.

Always looking for that unique image wherever I am helps me stay focused on my presence and the present. I gain a greater appreciation for the beauty of my surroundings. Reviewing my photos, editing the selected photos, and creating prints or photo books allows me to constantly relive the special experiences of my life. Obviously, I seldom travel anywhere without a camera in hand.

Because of my parents' love for boating and my spending summer weekends on Lake Erie—and with a name like "Seaman"—

water recreation activities remained an important part of my life. When I was offered the opportunity to go sailing in the Bahamas, this challenging sport quickly became a personal passion.

Sailing the Great Lakes, the East Coast, the Bahamas, and the Caribbean has been a rich reward for my family, my business associates, and for me personally. It is perhaps the best recreational activity that has helped Judy and me escape the "fast lane" of our very busy lives. As I often describe, my favorite part of sailing is "anchorage and a bottle of Grey Goose."

"You Cannot Do It All"

I recognize the constant challenge of trying to achieve and sustain balance among the many choices for allocating your time. This is particularly challenging when you have a strong passion for your career.

Not long ago I hired my son-in-law, the husband of our second daughter and the father of three of our granddaughters, to come to work for me. Although they lived in Wooster, Ohio, he had been working for a company in Chicago, which required monthly weeklong trips to the home office as well as many long hours in his office at home. I offered him the opportunity with our family business because of the unique skills he brought to our current needs. I also felt it would allow him to have more time to spend with his family.

During his first year of employment, I assigned him a project that would require about 50 percent of his time—namely, to oversee the construction and start up of the six-court indoor tennis facility for our associates and the community. Because of his passion for both the business opportunity as well as the sport of tennis itself, however, within months I found him spending 110 percent of his time on the project!

During a weekend when my wife and I were watching our three granddaughters, I heard them lament, "Daddy's been working a lot of long hours lately." Obviously, I took that as a clue to have a heart-to-heart talk with my son-in-law and share with him my thoughts and experiences on achieving a quality of life balance.

Giving priority to maintaining balance in your life actually supports and improves your ability to be a creative leader of the family business. I recall shortly after my father's death, while we still owned his 48' motor yacht, I decided to have the captain take me tarpon fishing for a few days on the southwest coast of Florida. At the time, I was struggling with some serious issues in the business. It would have been an easy decision for me to forgo this fishing vacation because of these pressing business issues.

But, I decided to disconnect for a few days and enjoyed some "downtime" relaxing on my father's boat. Obviously, the business issues were always in the back of my mind. Being able to let these issues and possible solutions "percolate" while enjoying the sunshine and warmth of southwest Florida actually allowed more creative ideas to develop. By the end of this much-needed break, I had developed a productive "plan of action" that would not have evolved had I stayed immersed in my day-to-day business environment.

Prioritize Your Personal Health

Given the experience I had with so many premature deaths of my family members and business associates early in my career, I placed a high priority on personal health habits. I was fortunate to read Dr. Ken Cooper's first book on aerobics. It instilled in me the value of exercise and its importance to a long-term healthy life. This motivated me to incorporate aerobic exercises into my health habits.

My wife and I also committed to executive physicals every year and a half to two years. In fact, many of those physicals were done at Dr. Cooper's clinic in Dallas, Texas. These regular physicals kept us informed of our personal health conditions and identified habits we needed to develop or continue to support a healthy lifestyle.

It is easy to sacrifice the time required for exercising or other health habits for business or family priorities. Just remember, however, that when you put at risk your personal health, you put at risk your family and your business. You will not be able to support either your family or your business needs if you become ill.

The investment in time and money in your personal health is by its very nature an investment in your ability to support your family and your business in a positive and productive way. By contrast, a serious health condition as a result of neglecting your health can be a significant burden on both your family and your business.

In my own case, these regular executive physicals identified an irregular heart rhythm that was resolved with a pacemaker (which I thought was only prescribed for old folks). Years later, an executive physical provided the early detection of prostate cancer, which was successfully treated with radioactive implants.

While both of these conditions were very concerning at the time they were diagnosed, these early treatment interventions successfully addressed the health conditions and have allowed me to continue an active lifestyle into my seventies.

Your Spouse and the Business

It is difficult to separate the growth and sustainability of a multi-generational family business from the importance of your spouse's involvement and support. In fact, in a survey conducted by Deutsche Bank in 2007, business owners rated their spouse as their most trusted confidante.[30]

While your spouse may or may not have a career in the family business, he or she is an invaluable asset and a compassionate ear to the many challenges you experience and express during your family business career. An understanding spouse will serve as a sounding board for your daily frustrations and, just as importantly, will celebrate the successes you will want to share.

Your spouse can help provide objective feedback and expand perspectives on the challenges you are facing. In addition, an involved spouse will help remind you of the importance of balance between your career, your marriage, and your relationship with your children.

An engaged and involved spouse helps put the "family" in a family business. Even if your spouse's career is not in the business, his or her presence and visibility among business associates highlights the "family" aspect of the family business. An engaged and involved spouse will play a very significant role in communicating both the treasure and the stewardship significance of a family business to the children and grandchildren—the future generation of owners.

As I reflect on the years of my growing up in a family business, I have such admiration for the role my mother played in supporting my father's passion. She was responsible for raising five children, beginning each morning by preparing a hearty breakfast before sending us off to school, and then spending a full workday managing the administrative functions of our young growing business.

Her responsibilities included managing the books and writing the checks to pay the bills. I know my father would have been unable to dedicate his creative time and skills to building the foundation of this family business and to raise a family of five children without the active and engaged support of his spouse.

In the case of my own spouse, Judy, she was at first hesitant to become involved in the family business, a role very unfamiliar and ill defined. And, given the family business issues with my mother and siblings following my father's death, there was even more reluctance.

Nonetheless, she was always there to listen to my challenges and frustrations as I attempted to resolve the family issues as well as the normal day-to-day business challenges. She also enjoyed sharing the successes of our business growth.

More importantly, once I purchased the business interests of my mother and siblings and began thinking about succession planning with our three children, Judy became very engaged in exploring family business ownership.

She was actively involved in the process of engaging our young children in the value and stewardship of owning a family business. She visited our manufacturing facilities regularly and, because of her love for gardening, was not afraid to roll up her sleeves and do the "dirty work" of weeding the front office landscaping areas. She participated in business social events with our associates and with our customers.

Judy has been very helpful in developing programs for our grandchildren that begin to teach them the value of owning a family business. Even though she does not have her career in the family business, the role she plays has a multidimensional impact on the success and sustainability of a multigenerational family business.

Never-ending Education

As a business continues to grow, it places new demands on its leadership and management team. It also places new demands on its ownership and family business leadership. A family business leader needs to commit to his or her own self-development process to meet the dynamic challenges of a growing business. If you are trying to grow your business but you are not growing yourself, it will likely not happen.

In 1967, I was recognized as one of the honor graduates of the College of Business at Bowling Green State University. To celebrate this recognition, the college sponsored a dinner for all honorees. Our featured speaker was the CEO of Sherwin Williams. By pure coincidence, I had the privilege of sitting next to our guest speaker during dinner.

In the course of our conversation, this CEO told me he was a member of the Young Presidents Organization. He said the organization was comprised of individuals who had become President of their companies before they were forty years old.

He spoke highly of this organization and its educational value to its members. Since I was joining my family business at the very young age of twenty-two, I visualized that someday I might qualify for membership in YPO.

Ten years later, after my father passed away and I was elected President of Seaman Corporation, I recalled that dinner conversation with the CEO of Sherwin Williams. I began researching membership requirements for YPO. Several years later, I applied and was selected for membership in the organization's Cleveland chapter.

As President of a small family business in the small community of Millersburg, Ohio, I viewed my membership in this prestigious organization as both opportunistic and intimidating. Nonetheless, I explored the YPO's many educational opportunities and participated in its social offerings.

YPO became an invaluable resource for me and for my family over the years. We attended local chapter events that sponsored excellent educational resources. We also attended YPO "universities," weeklong educational programs, many of which were family focused. The quality of the resources and programs at both the local and the international level supported YPO's motto: "Better Presidents through Education."

Participating in the variety of excellent educational programs offered by YPO became a mental recharge for me and further developed my personal growth. The highlight of this educational opportunity was my attendance at the annual YPO Presidents Program on Leadership at the Harvard Business School. I referred to this program as YPO Boot Camp.

Each year I attended YPO Boot Camp I not only enhanced my business leadership skills but also brought back lessons and ideas to share with my leadership team. I also connected with many resources that we subsequently used to support the educational and training initiatives with our management team. This was where I met my Korean classmate (described in the introduction) who underscored the importance of stewardship that accompanies the privilege of family business ownership.

These learning experiences became an important part of our business growth strategies. In addition, I identified and recruited two very valuable members for our outside board of directors through the associations I developed while attending these HBS programs.

While I was fortunate to have the educational opportunities offered by the Young Presidents Organization as my primary source of self-development, many other educational offerings are also available. Virtually every major graduate business school offers one-week continuing education programs for executives on a wide range of business topics. And a number of organizations other than YPO, like Vistage, Business Network International (BNI), Young Entrepreneur Council (YEC), or Entrepreneurs' Organization (EO), recruit and support small groups of corporate CEOs to meet on a regular basis and share their leadership challenges.

Personal self-development is a key component to sustaining yourself and your leadership capability for growing a multigenerational family business. In other words,

Know thyself

Personal growth and development requires self-reflection during your leadership journey. In the mid-1980s, when I asked our board member who was a psychologist and organizational development consultant what he thought I could do to improve my leadership, I was very surprised when he suggested that I attend a Gestalt-sponsored Men's Weekend Workshop. I took the risk of enrolling in this course, despite the fact that this board member was going to be one of the facilitators and, as I later learned, one of my best friends would also be participating. This was a most unusual experience for me and encouraged me to be mentally and emotionally vulnerable.

In addition, I have found that consultants trained in Gestalt therapy have been some of the most beneficial to me personally and professionally. Participating in the Gestalt process taught me the importance of developing an awareness of what is truly happening in the present, whether that be with the group or with me personally. What is the reality of the situation, separate and apart from the specific content? What is occurring within me, both emotionally and physically, separate and apart from the situation?

At the basic level, Gestalt simply recognizes and builds on inherent human nature that has been a part of each of us for centuries. As such, it enables us to diffuse the intensity of our emotions and redirect our emotional energy to the more authentic forces that are impacting us, both externally and internally.

Perhaps the most significant factor for self-sustenance while growing a family business is the personal passion you have for the business. This leadership role will not be a career of joy if you do not have a love for the products or services, a love for the associates, a love for the customers, and an appreciation for the value your business creates. Otherwise, your career will be little more than a chore.

It is important to recognize that the culture of the family business enterprise will be a reflection of the passion of its leader. It will be difficult to create a business organization that has a multigenerational culture if the leader is operating the business for his or her own lifestyle or if the organization perceives the leader's involvement as simply working through the daily grind.

Because a business organization is a reflection of the personality and value system of the leader, it is important for the leader to be an optimist. Every business organization will face challenging times because of changing and unpredictable economic conditions. An organization will be much more responsive to these challenging times when it sees and hears a leader who is realistic but optimistic about the ability of its associates to navigate through the choppy waters ahead.

Our business today continues to reflect the legacy and culture that my father embedded in our foundation. He had a passion for innovation and research and development, from mixing chemicals in my mother's kitchen to creating fabrics for air support structures or inflatable boats. His never-ending quest for developing better industrial fabrics for a multitude of heavy-duty applications continues to drive the culture for innovation and R&D in our company today, even though it is fifteen times larger than when he passed away forty years ago.

I am fortunate to share a great deal of my father's passion for our business. The continuing growth of Seaman Corporation and the continuing growth of our leadership team and all our associates give me an incredible sense of accomplishment and self-fulfillment. Continued business and personal growth have always been a message I have tried to convey. A culture of growth, supported by improving the processes required to drive that growth, is what I believe will create a multigenerational family business.

I felt very gratified when we achieved our first $50 million in annual sales in 1994, nearly fifty years after my father started the company. I wanted to celebrate this achievement with all our associates and did so by personally handing each associate a commemorative plaque that included a crisp new $50 bill.

When I made these presentations, I congratulated the entire organization on achieving the sales results and said I could not wait until I had the opportunity to hand them a plaque containing a crisp new $100 bill. Much to my own surprise, I was able to do so ten years later, in 2004, when we achieved our first $100 million in annual sales.

Then, in 2016, I was also very gratified to hand each associate a commemorative plaque containing three $50 bills to celebrate our first $150 million in annual sales the same year that I retired after forty years as CEO of Seaman Corporation. Celebrating these growth milestones with the team of associates that helped achieve these incredible results is one of the self-sustaining elements that continues to reflect my passion for our family business.

A successful growing business reflects the culture and passion of its founder. Successful multigenerational family businesses reflect the legacy of many leaders. Each generational leader has the opportunity to put his or her thumbprint on this legacy. Each generation, however, must recognize the legacy of the previous leaders.

When passing leadership on to future generations, it is also important not to constrain them with your particular passion or leadership style. You should congratulate the next generation and remind them of the unique and tremendous opportunity of stewarding a family treasure that allows them to develop their passion. One of the treasures of a family business is that it provides a platform that will support a variety of passions. But, at the same time, you must be mindful that it will impact not only their lives but also the lives of the many associates and their families who are working for the family business.

Accepting a leadership role in a multigenerational family business can be overwhelming, so it is important to maintain a long-term strategic view. Remember that the journey is a marathon, not a sprint. While you may have a vision for your finish line, it will be difficult to anticipate each mile marker along the way. Many unpredictable factors will affect your race and will impact the time and the course it takes to get to your finish line.

Having a passion for your business, its products and services, its customers and associates; staying focused on your self-development; achieving balance in your priorities; and, above all, remaining optimistic about crossing your visionary finish line are requisite to sustaining yourself during this marathon journey.

Twenty years from now you will be more disappointed by the things that you didn't do than by the ones you did do. So throw off the bowlines. Sail away from the safe harbor. Catch the trade winds in your sails. Explore. Dream. Discover.

—Mark Twain

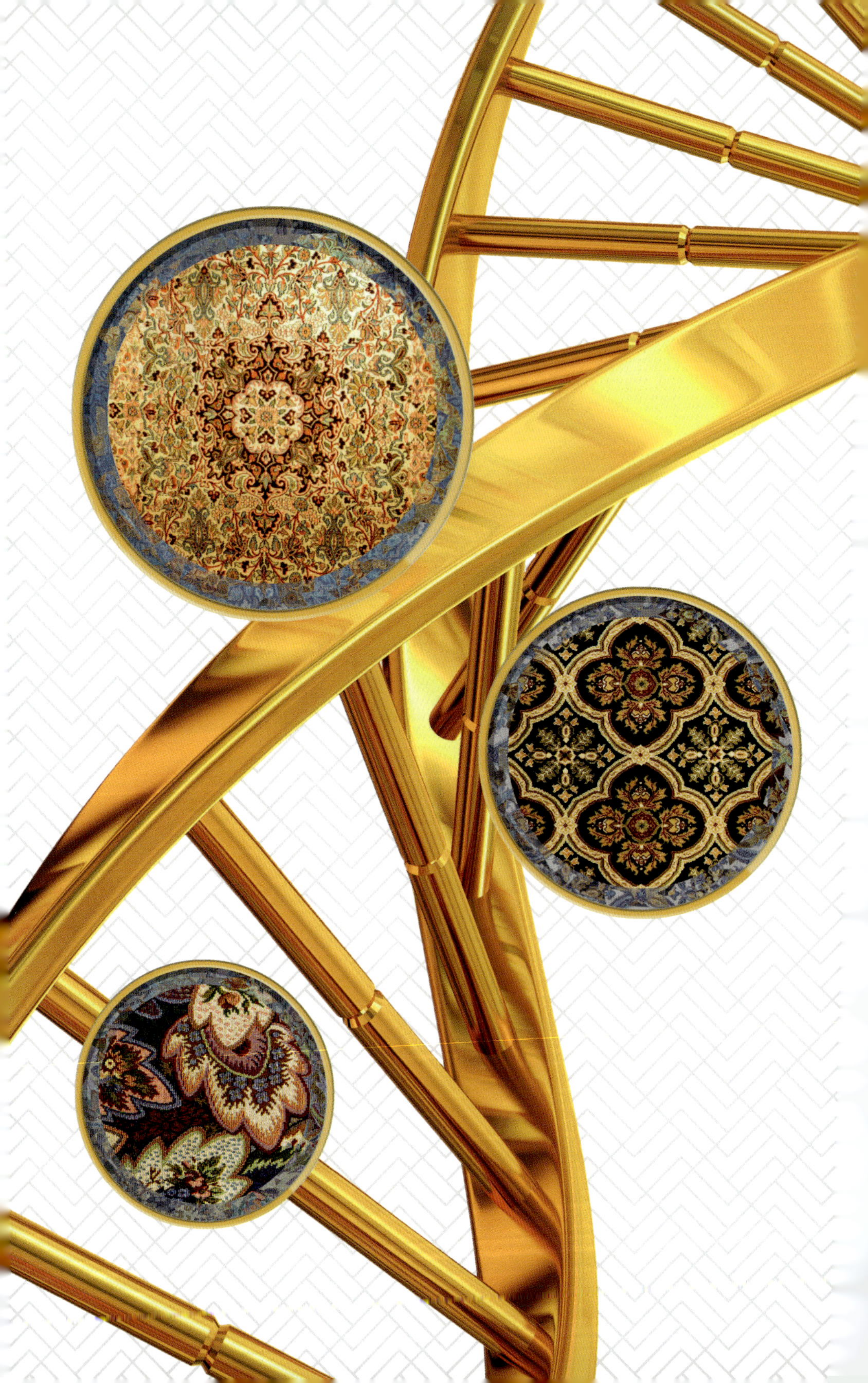

CONCLUSION

A LASTING LEGACY

*In America, family-owned businesses represent
the essential threads of our economy.*

We have seen the vast amount of data that confirms the significant contribution family businesses make to our economy. Family businesses are the job creators in our economy. Innovation and new ideas emerge from family businesses. Customers trust products and services produced by family businesses. Employees prefer working for family businesses.

Family businesses have unique cultures that cultivate principles of stewardship and community philanthropy. These values embedded in family businesses are a strong component of our culture.

Family business values such as innovation, work ethic, strong customer and supplier relationships, and dedication to associates, to mention a few, strengthen our culture and society. These are only reinforced when the business enterprise follows a multigenerational path.

Recognizing and celebrating these values will have a positive effect on influencing public policy that will help create and sustain an economic ecosystem that supports innovation and entrepreneurship. It will value the principles of capitalism, which are the basis for our growing and resilient economy.

> *If we created a society that valued and facilitated multigenerational family businesses, we would shift the focus of our economy to supporting innovation, entrepreneurship, and job creation with less focus on creating a finance-centric economy.*

We are a country that births an abundance of family-owned businesses. This plethora of family businesses reflects our entrepreneurial spirit and our "rugged individualism." We have an inherent desire to work for ourselves and not be dependent on others for our livelihood. This individualism motivates us to operate our own businesses, even though it may require more hours and provide less financial reward. We value the freedom to weave our own tapestry of life.

Family-owned businesses exist for a multitude of reasons. A vast majority of these businesses are single proprietorships, providing for the day-to-day economic well-being of the owners and their families. As family businesses enjoy successful growth, the value created is often used to support the ever-increasing lifestyle of its owners and their families.

Many family business owners hope to pass the business on to their children, but only if one or more of their children commit their careers to the business. If no family descendants are willing to work in the business, the owner explores an exit strategy.

In most cases, the exit strategy is to sell the business. The vast amount of capital available through our private equity industry, combined with our efficient market economy and the abundance of investment bankers, easily facilitates monetizing the value that has been created over time in a family business. As a result, family business owners, having toiled most of their career, are motivated to take advantage of a private equity liquidity opportunity when they do not have a son or daughter who wants a career in the business, or if they simply are not organized enough to effectively manage a succession transition.

While the owner is well rewarded for his or her years of leadership and work, those employees who have helped the business achieve this value seldom share in this liquidation event. In most cases, these employees work hard for the next owner primarily to generate cash flow that gets allocated to the payments required for the debt that was used to leverage the purchase—only to be sold again to another private equity firm. Oftentimes the debt burden becomes too great for the business and the jobs vanish during its demise.

Because of these traditional journeys of family businesses, our culture gives little attention to the concept of growing multigenerational family-owned businesses. We generally think of family businesses lasting only two to three generations. The entrepreneurship models that are promulgated today focus on start-up, a journey through phases of financing, followed by a liquidation exit—usually in less than one generation.

The family-owned businesses that are successfully passed on to future generations represent true treasures for our economy and for our country. They have institutionalized meaningful values. By necessity, they have to be innovative. They contribute significantly to our economy and to job creation. Most play an important philanthropic role in their communities. We would do well as a society to recognize and celebrate the entrepreneurship embedded in these businesses—an entrepreneurship model of "higher calling."

Unfortunately, less than 5 percent of family businesses succeed at being multigenerational. This is primarily because most founders and second-generation leaders of family businesses are not familiar with how to approach the challenges of multigenerational ownership.

Creating and managing a growing business in today's economy presents many challenges. There is global competition. We constantly experience unpredictable changing economic conditions. Public policy is not supportive with its abundance of government regulations and estate tax laws that constrain our ability to pass family businesses on to the next generation.

To have a vision for and commit to this higher calling by creating and growing a family business for multigenerational succession is a significant challenge, yes; but it is also a rewarding treasure and lasting legacy.

I have experienced most of these challenges as a second-generation owner and CEO of an industrial fabric business that grew from $2 million to $175 million in annual sales and will be passed on to the third generation. I will be forever grateful to my father and mother for their enduring commitment to start a business in the basement of our home that became the foundation for our family business.

I attribute my success in growing this business to the capable leadership of many dedicated associates, to the commitment of a dedicated board, and to family shareholders who want to be stewards of our family business. We all worked together to identify important business processes that we were willing to adopt and effectively implement throughout our family enterprise.

I am confident that the business processes I have described in this book will be valuable tools to any family business owners who have the vision to grow their business with the desire to pass the family enterprise on to future generations. And I believe this continuing legacy will be far more rewarding than a liquidation event that is not shared by all who helped achieve the business success.

Public company boards have been led to believe that their first and foremost responsibility is to make decisions that are in the best interest of the shareholders. Customer interests and employee interests are secondary.

I have seen too many times when board decisions are justified because they are in the best interest of the shareholders to maximize their current returns. These decisions may actually be harmful to the customers and employees, which ultimately results in the demise of the business.

Successful multigenerational family-owned businesses, public or private, will make their decisions first and foremost for the customer, next for the employees. In my opinion, if these decisions are executed well, the company will thrive and the shareholders will do well because of the sustainable value creation that is accomplished.

The creation and growth of a family business for multigenerational purposes is responding to a higher calling. A growing multigenerational family-owned business will maintain existing job employment and will create new future jobs. The business can also serve as a platform for ongoing philanthropy.

As our family business grew, my wife and I created a family foundation. As the company became more financially successful, the family shareholders and the board agreed to distribute 5 percent of its after-tax earnings to the family foundation. Family members make decisions on grants to support philanthropic causes that are consistent with the mission of the foundation. Company associates are aware that a portion of the profits are distributed to the philanthropic foundation, further supporting the culture of the company.

Over the past two decades, our company has been contributing its outdated inventory of industrial fabrics to two nongovernment organizations: Friendships International and World Vision. These two NGOs have successfully utilized our fabrics for a variety of humanitarian causes around the world. In more than twenty-five countries, Seaman fabrics have been used for emergency shelters during hurricane and earthquake disasters. Housing, for instance, for Somalian refugees and as a medical clinic for Syrian refugees. Instead of being sold at significantly discounted prices or simply shipped to a landfill, these fabrics continue to support humanitarian causes and serve as a special source of pride for all our associates.

Every business owner has the opportunity to determine the future of his or her business enterprise. While there is always the incentive to focus on an exit strategy that monetizes the equity value, there is also the option to have the enterprise become a lasting legacy for future family generations. Future descendants do not have to commit their careers in the business but *do* need to be willing to be active stewards of the family business. Should that be your decision, you and your family must make deliberate strategic choices that will support multigenerational growth.

There are many organizations and associations available throughout the country that support family businesses, including the opportunity to network with other family businesses facing similar challenges. Only a few, like the Family Business Network, the Family Business Consulting Group, EY Family Business Services, and Egon Zehnder, focus on multigenerational family businesses.

Rotating a kaleidoscope presents an infinite variety of colorful patterns, not unlike the life choices we all have. If you have the opportunity to choose a pattern that reflects the colorful entrepreneurship and unique DNA of a family business, you are blessed with being the steward of a true treasure.

ACKNOWLEDGMENT AND APPRECIATION

For many years, I contemplated the idea of writing a book—perhaps a dream that many entrepreneurs have near the end of their careers. But when I would think about the possibility, it seemed like a daunting task.

While I believed my career and life experiences contained many stories that might fill the pages of a book, I wondered if the dream was simply a catharsis for validating self-worth, which in and of itself might justify the lengthy process. But I wanted my effort to provide learnings for others and to be both inspirational and helpful to the entrepreneurial spirit. And I did not simply want to repeat what others had already eloquently penned—not just be a coat of another color.

In 2017, my close friend Pat Finley completed this courageous task and published his book, *Spinning into Control*. He quickly connected me with his writing consultant, Kelsey Grode. *A Vibrant Vision* exists today because of the encouragement and research capability of Kelsey. She spent time with me probing my ideas and immediately began researching the literature. While she found many books written about how to grow a company and many books about family businesses, she believed there was vacant space for a book that addressed how to grow a business specifically with the intent of passing it on to future generations.

From there, we were off and running—for the next two and a half years! Kelsey spent weeks interviewing me to capture my ideas. Her outlines and notes from these interviews were invaluable to my writing process. During this journey, Kelsey was my enthusiastic cheerleader, keeping me on task and properly focused. Her knowledge of the book writing process facilitated all the elements required to not only produce a manuscript but also to present it to the reader in a compelling manner. After many memorable visits from her California home to join us in Wooster, Ohio, or Beaver Creek, Colorado, Judy and I began referring to Kelsey as our adopted West Coast daughter.

The ideas in this book have been inspired by many special people that have been a part of my life and my career. Of course, my father and mother, Norm and Irene Seaman, head this list. They had the courage and fortitude to start a business in the basement of their home in 1949 not only for their family's economic survival but also with the unspoken vision of creating career opportunities for their five children.

I owe a great deal of appreciation to John Ward, a family business consultant I met shortly after my father passed away in 1978. Our paths did not cross again until nearly twenty years later, during which time John had conducted research on more than 5,000 family businesses from around the world. I had recently completed purchasing my family's interest in our family business and was trying to visualize succession planning at a time when my children did not have any desire to work in the family business. John's research led him to creating the concept of "active shareholders" and this became the basis for developing our family business succession plan. John became an invaluable consultant to both my family and our board of directors as we began our journey of multigenerational succession planning.

After my father passed away, I made the fortunate decision to join the Young Presidents Organization, whose mission is "Better Presidents through Education." This organization offered both me and my family incredible ongoing educational opportunities through unique programming, such as YPO "universities" and the YPO Harvard Presidents Program. These educational experiences became the basis for many of the business processes that are presented in *A Vibrant Vision*.

The Family Business Network is an international organization of more than 3,300 family businesses. Our family's membership in this organization provided me with a unique exposure to multigenerational family businesses from around the world. These experiences reinforced the unique importance family businesses play in both the economies and the cultures of the world.

Another fortunate decision I made after my father passed away was to create an independent outside board of directors. I owe a great deal of gratitude to the family business consultant Leon Danco and his guidance on selecting independent directors.

As a result of Leon's early guidance, Seaman Corporation has been blessed with many qualified independent directors over the decades. These well-respected individuals have been invaluable to my leadership teams and, more importantly, to my family members. They have been a positive challenge to me in my CEO leadership role for forty years and have supported my family as they engaged in the unique responsibilities of multigenerational family business ownership.

I owe a great deal to the Seaman Corporation leadership teams. Growing a business over many decades requires the support of talented leadership teams. I have been fortunate to attract management talent that have willingly engaged in creating change initiatives that have built the business process infrastructure required to sustain the growth of our business for generations to come.

And then there are the many resources that were instrumental in evolving my written manuscript into an attractive and (hopefully) inspirational book. Linda O'Doughda provided thoughtful and thorough input during her copyedit of the manuscript. David Ruffo and Debbie Kennedy of Seich Ruffo Graphic Design, along with illustrator Terry Paczko, utilized their creative skills to develop the graphics in the book and to design the layout for the printer.

Tim Godek, our Seaman Corporation Graphic Designer, researched our photography archives and provided most of the product photos used in the book.

And speaking of photography, I appreciate the excellent photographic skills of my friend Peter Nash. Many of the corporate and product photos were created by Peter. More importantly, he has inspired and taught me a great deal that has enhanced my personal photography hobby—offering a significant colorful component to my kaleidoscope of life.

I want to give special recognition and thanks to my wife, Judy, and our daughters, Carrie and Kim. While perhaps not as obvious, their willingness to read the manuscript provided unique and invaluable input for improving the family stories that support the evolution of our family business ownership experiences.

APPENDIX A
Seaman Corporation Corporate Philosophy

Mission Statement:

Seaman Corporation is committed to advancing the state of the art in the design, manufacture, and utilization of industrial fabrics, films, and coatings by integrating its weaving, compounding, coating, and applied fabric engineering technologies to satisfy the product and service requirements of its customers.

Corporate Values:

The values that govern Seaman Corporation will engender a simultaneous consideration of the goals and desires of all who are a part of its success: its family of customers, employees, suppliers, owners, and community members.

We will foster and promote planned, controlled growth characterized by an obsession for product quality and customer service. Our behavior in the business community will be marked by a dedication to high integrity, honesty, total customer satisfaction, and fairness in value. We will strive to establish long-lasting and mutually beneficial relationships with both customers and suppliers.

Our organization will be structured in ways which will encourage our employees to grow with us while they achieve their career aspirations. We will require creativity, innovation, initiative, and employee involvement. Employees at all levels will be responsible for on-going training and development. Generating opportunities for the career development of our employees will be an important part of our Strategic Quality Planning Process.

Seaman Corporation will seek recognition as a quality-driven organization in its products, its service, and its people. It will be characterized by quality and service responsiveness in the marketplace, informality and openness in the workplace, and a sense of corporate pride in its history and accomplishments.

A VIBRANT VISION

Guiding Principles:

Seaman Corporation has emerged as a dynamic, successful business entity by adhering to several basic principles. These elements will continue to guide the future of the Company as it grows and prospers. They will also provide a set of standards against which any major policy decision will be evaluated.

We therefore seek to maintain:

...total customer satisfaction in the products and services we provide.

...a corporate closeness to the customer which will provide product performance and service that meets or exceeds customer requirements.

...an emphasis on innovative product and service development and the degree of vertical integration necessary to insure the premium value our customers expect from us.

...integrity and honesty in our business relationships with our customers, our employees our suppliers, and the business community as a whole.

...a safe work environment which will attract and retain excellent employees and will encourage and enable them to develop professionally and personally with equal opportunity.

...an informal work climate and fairness in our employee relations practices where all employees participate in decision-making activities and are recognized for their team and individual contributions.

...profitable growth objectives which will provide reasonable returns to our shareholders, reinvestment capital to our organization, and new challenges to our employees, and

...a positive presence in and sustained support for the communities in which we and our employees, suppliers, customers, and shareholders reside.

Richard N. Seaman
Chairman of the Board

APPENDIX B
Governance and Leadership Structure

As part of the periodic review of leadership succession planning, Seaman Corporation (the Company) has adopted a new Leadership Structure. This document reflects the work of the Company's Board of Directors and the active Seaman Family Shareholders. It has been developed to strengthen the Company's future leadership at a particularly important time with the anticipated retirement of long-time CEO, Chairman and Family Shareholder, Richard N. Seaman.

The new governance and leadership structure includes the following: a CEO, Non-Executive Chairman of the Board, an Executive Committee of the Board, the Board of Directors, and the Seaman Family Shareholders. This structure allows for the position of CEO to be separate from the position of Chairman of the Board, and to be filled by the most qualified leader for the Company, including individuals outside the Family Shareholder group. The structure also allows and encourages qualified Seaman Family Shareholders to take part in the leadership of the Company, supporting the CEO, through significant interaction with the Board of Directors.

The following document serves to: define the new structure of leadership, clarify the major aspects of each leader's roles, and identify the target qualities sought when assessing an individual's qualifications to fill these roles. Along with the text, the accompanying illustration aims to demonstrate the relationships between and among the individuals participating in the model. Additionally, a matrix at the end of the document demonstrates how each leader or group is involved in major decisions that affect the Company.

This Leadership Structure will be in effect at the time of the retirement of Richard N. Seaman and is subject to modification by the Board of Directors at any time deemed necessary.

APPENDIX B (Continued)

CEO

MAJOR ASPECTS OF ROLE:

Ensure Alignment with Shareholder and Board

Ensure the (1) achievement of a reasonable interpretation of the organizational results, beneficiaries, and costs of those results described in Shareholder "Statement of Purpose and Future Expectations" and Board Governance Policies, and (2) avoidance of unacceptable conditions and actions described in the Shareholder "Statement of Purpose and Future Expectations" and Board Governance Policies.

Make all decisions, create all policies, and authorize all engagements that are consistent with a reasonable interpretation of Shareholder Expectations and Board policies.

Maintain on-going dialogue with the Chairman of the Board and the Executive Committee

Strategic Leadership

Develop and implement strategy reflecting short- and long-term objectives and priorities established by the Board and Shareholders.

Build and maintain an effective executive team (SLT), including ensuring succession planning for the CEO and all SLT positions.

Operational/Managerial Leadership

Develop and maintain effective operational planning and financial control systems.

Closely monitor operating and financial results in accordance with plans and budgets.

Assume full accountability to the Board for all aspects of company operations and performance.

Representing the Company

Represent the company to key entities, including major customers, industry leaders, the unity, and political leaders.

TARGET QUALITIES:

Values
Integrity
Carrier of family values
    Value and respect the culture

Strategic Leadership
Strategic thinker and implementer
    Able to anticipate three moves ahead
Can lead innovation
Able to make tough decisions in a timely way

Relational and Communication Skills
Leader of change
    Very effective interpersonally
        Calm
        Consultative, inclusive/transparent, people person
        Has deep external networks and capability to develop more
Effective communicator sufficient to be spokesperson for the company
    Able to articulate ideas

Knowledgeable
Deep knowledge of business and industry
Able to understand/articulate Seaman's technology platforms and related platforms
Engaged in industry as a whole
Data driven
Sales capable

Creative Intelligence
Intelligent
    Curious; open to experience
    Learner
Non-linear thinking
    Capable of divergent and lateral thinking
    Capable of understanding complexity of causes and effects
Systems thinker
    Able to go global and adapt to very different ways of doing business

Modeling
Workhorse
Ability to motivate and inspire

APPENDIX B (Continued)

Chairman Of The Board (Non-Executive)
MAJOR ASPECTS OF ROLE:

Strategic Oversight

Ensure that the CEO and SLT conduct an effective, comprehensive strategic planning process resulting in effective strategy and direction that is in alignment with active shareholder expectations.

Ensure that the Board effectively reviews, adds value to, and ultimately approves the company's strategy and direction in alignment with active shareholder expectations.

CEO Relationship

Maintain close contact with the CEO so as to be aware of major business issues and context.

Ensure effective goal setting for and assessment of the CEO by the board.

Leadership of Board

Ensure monitoring and appropriate updating of the structure and composition of the Board and Executive Committee.

Plan Board and Executive Committee meetings and agendas.

Ensure the Board receives proper information.

Chair all Board and Executive Committee meetings.

Ensure that all matters discussed and agreed to by the Board are properly captured and recorded.

Support open discussion and consensus building.

Ensure that all Board members are engaged and contribute.

Help the Board fulfill its goals by assigning specific tasks to members of the Board.

Ensure effective goal setting and assessment of Board Members.

Company Representation

Serve as the primary spokesperson for the Board.

Together with the CEO represents the company to external entities.

TARGET QUALITIES:

Values Driven
Integrity
    Carrier of family values
Understanding of the best practices in family business governance

Business Acumen
With support from the Executive Committee, capable of mentoring the CEO
Solid understanding of the business
    Capable of backing up the CEO and/or ensuring backup of CEO

Evaluative Skills
Capable of leading the process by which the board evaluates the CEO
Capable of leading the process of Board self-evaluation
Capable of leading the process for CEO recruitment

Relational Skills
Strong leadership skills
Teamwork skills
Capable of respecting the boundaries of the CEO
Strong interpersonally
    Solid relationships with key parties
Being a family member would be preferential (if one is available)

APPENDIX B (Continued)

Executive Committee
Major Aspects of Role:

Strategic Oversight

Take the lead in ensuring that the CEO and SLT conduct an effective, comprehensive strategic planning process resulting in effective strategy and direction that is in alignment with active shareholder expectations.

Take the lead in ensuring that the Board effectively reviews, adds value to, and ultimately approves the company's strategy and direction in alignment with active shareholder expectations.

CEO and Chair Relationships

Maintain solid contact with the CEO and the Chair so as to be aware of major business issues and context.

Provide counsel to the CEO and the Chair that helps build understanding and support effective decision making.

Support effective goal setting for and Board assessment of the CEO.

Work with the Chair to assure mentoring capability for the CEO.

Providing Backup

Step up to the plate if Chair decides to step down (at least one designated Executive Committee member).

Develop, maintain, and review with Active Shareholders and the Board a list of potential candidates for Director positions.

TARGET QUALITIES:

Values Driven
Honest, ethical

Gives priority to the best interests of family, shareholders, and employees (more important than business skills)

Business Acumen
Strong business experience, background
    Strong financial knowledge
        Ability to give counsel in a wide range of business issues

Solid understanding of the business

At least one member of the Executive Committee capable of mentoring the CEO

Potential to backup CEO and/or ensuring backup of CEO (at least one member of the Executive Committee)

Relational Skills
Strong leadership skills

Teamwork skills

Independent Thinking
Being out-of-the-box thinkers and not inclined to group-think

Willingness to candidly engage with the Chair and the CEO

Committed
Engaged
    Makes commitment of time

Available
    Responsive

APPENDIX B (Continued)

BOARD
MAJOR ASPECTS OF ROLE:

Values

Promote and conserve the Seaman culture, values, and legacy.

Act in good faith in the best interest of the Company toward shareholders, employees, customers, and communities.

Understand and ensure alignment with the "Statement of Purpose and Future Expectations" of the Active Shareholder Group.

Strategic Oversight

Review, challenge, and approve the strategic plan, support the approved plan, and review and approve any major changes in strategy.

Review, challenge, evaluate and decide on major capital projects and acquisitions (referring analysis to shareholders above designated thresholds).

Review, challenge, and evaluate, mergers and changes of control of the corporation prior to referring to shareholders.

Ask questions and review information to ensure understanding of major issues.

Operational Oversight

Create an atmosphere of accountability.

Provide oversight and feedback on financial and operational performance and guide corrective action when necessary.

Review and oversee the corporation's management of risk; ensure compliance with ethical and legal standards.

CEO/Officer Relationship

Provide thoughtful, relevant counsel to the CEO on various aspects of the business.

Elect the CEO and other officers of the company.

Establish performance goals for the CEO and other senior executives.

Review CEO performance.

Decide on CEO compensation.

Develop, approve, and implement succession plans for the CEO and other top executives.

Board Engagement

Become familiar with responsibilities, rights, and duties of directorship.

Prepare for and fully participate in Board and committee meetings.

Help identify and recruit new Board candidates in collaboration with the Active Shareholder Group and, if needed, appoint Interim Directors when there are vacancies.

Company Representation

Represent the corporation well in the community.

TARGET QUALITIES:

Values Driven

Integrity; honors commitments

Values and respects Seaman culture and legacy

Has concern and consideration for all stakeholders, including shareholders, employees, customers, and communities

Avoids any possibility of conflict of interest

Strategic Oversight

Understanding of and experience with strategy formation and strategic planning as a process

Able to think strategically
> Looks ahead at unseen consequences, knows trends, and is future oriented

Business Acumen

High-level previous management experience; broad business background; ability to give counsel on many aspects of business

Able to develop knowledge of all aspects of the Seaman Corporation business, its technology platforms, and industries in which it participates

Understanding of Roles/Boundaries

Understanding of the roles of each level of leadership: Board, Executive Committee, Chairman (Non-Executive), CEO, and SLT

Diagnostic
> Able to ask management informed questions to gain better comprehension of the issue, but not to tell management how to do their job

Independent, Constructive Thinking

Inquiring and independent mind, practical wisdom (common sense), and mature judgment

Able to offer opinions honestly, collaboratively, and constructively and provide a different, non-conforming perspective to help the board avoid groupthink. Able to influence other strong minded individuals but also able to change positions, given appropriate information

Relational Skills

Treats other people and their opinions with respect, acts in a courteous and professional manner, keeps emotions under control.

Promotes unity within the company; supports board decisions (internally and externally) even when disagreeing with the majority opinion

Complementary

Background and skills that complement other board members'

APPENDIX B (Continued)

ACTIVE SHAREHOLDER GROUP
MAJOR ASPECTS OF ROLE:

Values

Promote and conserve the Seaman culture, values, and legacy.

Act in good faith in the best interest of the Company toward employees, customers, all shareholders, and communities.

Understand and ensure alignment with the "Statement of Purpose and Future Expectations" of the Active Shareholder Group.

Governance/Shareholder Coordination

Stay informed of and implement family business governance best practices.

Ensure the clear definition, maintenance, and development of an Active Shareholder Group.

Attend and participate in relevant meetings and committees.

Elect board members (in conjunction with a majority of all shareholders).

Review and approve capital expenditures that have a greater than 3-5 year payback.

Review, challenge, evaluate, and decide on major acquisitions, mergers, divestitures, and change of control.

Promote/Communicate Seaman Culture/Values and Expectations

Define, preserve, and promote the history, culture, and legacy of the family and company by supporting, advocating for, and assuring adherence to the Mission, Values, and Guiding Principles of the Corporate Philosophy.

Establish, communicate and monitor adherence to the Active Shareholder Group's major expectations related to company performance.

Maintain effective lines of communications with other shareholders, the Board, management, and associates.

Knowledgeable Stewardship

Develop and maintain knowledge about business and industry issues.

Serve as a steward of the assets of the company.

Company Representation

Represent the company in a positive manner in the community.

Support the communities in which the company operates.

TARGET QUALITIES:

Age/Family
Be a Seaman family member (as defined in the Seaman Family Governance Manual)

Be at least 18 years of age

Engagement
Engaged with the Board
     Makes commitment of time

Available and responsive

Willing to learn and listen

Responsible Stewardship
Uphold and support the Code of Conduct as specified in the Seaman Family Governance Manual

Understands the roles and responsibilities that come with ownership

Views the family business as an asset worth preserving for future generations

Strives for positive relationships with other shareholders

As a representative of the family, uphold a standard of professionalism

APPENDIX C
Care Quality Commitment (CQC)
Our Never-Ending Quest for World-Class Excellence

CUSTOMERS ARE THE REASON FOR EXCELLENCE
LEADERSHIP PRINCIPLES

Visible Quality Leadership

Obsession with the Customer

Uncompromising Integrity

Respect for People

Strong "Bias for Action" Toward Total Quality Improvement

A Positive Presence in, and Sustained Support for, the Community, Public Health and Safety, and the Environment

Commitment to Continual Innovation by the Pursuit of Never-ending Improvement in All Value-Added Business Processes

Total Performance Continually Measured Against "Best-In-Class"

Superior Return on Assets Employed (ROAE)

100% TOTAL CUSTOMER SATISFACTION

The customer has a right to expect:
Product Performance Features That Provide Fair Value

Product and Service That Is Delivered When Promised

Product That Is Delivered with No Defects

Product That Meets or Exceeds Expected Performance Requirements

Continually Strive to Exceed Customer Expectations and "Create Value" for the Customer by:
Listening to the Customer

Anticipating Customer Requirements

Identifying Customer Critical Success Factors (CSF)
    What we must do well to win the order
    What we must do well to keep the customer
    What gives us a sustainable long-term advantage

Imagine Responsiveness to the Customer

100% On-Time Delivery

Product and Service Quality Which Meets or Exceeds End-Use Performance Requirements

Timely Responsiveness to Customer Complaints

Courtesy to the Customer at All Times

100% Total Customer Satisfaction Involves Both External and Internal Customers

QUALITY PRINCIPLES

Committed to the Principle of Never-ending Improvement
Continual Improvement for Total Quality Is the Most Important Strategic Competitive Weapon

Improved Quality Will Gain the Largest Market Share, Provide the Highest Return on Assets Employed, and in the Long Run, Achieve the Lowest Possible Cost

Quality Results Apply to the Performance of All Value-Added Processes

Continually Measure Performance Against "Best-In-Class

Customer Service	People Development
Marketing	Manufacturing
Product Quality	Technology
Information Systems	Support Services

Committed to Achieving "Best-In-Class" Standards in All Value-Added Processes

Measurement Systems Will Utilize Benchmarking, Statistical Process Control and Trend Analysis

APPENDIX C (Continued)

COMPETITIVE ADVANTAGE REQUIRES EXCELLENCE
STRATEGIC QUALITY PLANNING PRINCIPLES

Strategic Quality Planning Is a Never-ending Business Process

The Planning Process Is Driven by CARE Quality Objectives Developed by:
  Customer Success Factors
 "Best-In-Class" Benchmarking of Value-Added Processes
  Competitive Analysis

Recognizes a Global Market Environment

Increase Global Market Share by Developing Product and Service Leadership

Accomplish Superior Financial Performance Results: 15% Pre-Tax Return on Assets Employed (ROAE)

DEVELOPMENT OF HUMAN RESOURCES

Empowerment of the People Unleashes the Total Potential of Our Organization

Priority Is Given to a Safe Working Environment

Requires Best-In-Class People Selection

Requires Best-In-Class Continual Training and Development

Focuses on Associate Well-Being and Morale

Total Associate Involvement Is Accomplished by:
   CARE Quality Improvement Teams
   Idea Implementation Process
   Associate Recognition Process
   Associate Customer Involvement
   Continual Improvement in Communication by Practicing the:

   Six Management Actions* © 1988 The Hertz Group
   1. Use positive reinforcement
   2. Ask what questions, problems, and concerns your people have and ask how you can help
   3. Ask for input prior to decision making
   4. Provide information and feedback in a timely manner
   5. Don't overmanage or undermanage
   6. Treat your people with respect

QUALITY ASSURANCE OF 100% TOTAL CUSTOMER SATISFACTION

100% Total Customer Satisfaction Drives the New Business Development Process for Both Product and Service

Total Quality Begins with the Product Design Process Partnership with the Customer to Understand End-Use Requirements
- Utilize Cross-Functional Teams in the Design Process
- Design for Manufacturability
- Partnership with Suppliers Throughout the Design and Commercialization Process

Continually Reduce Process Cycle Time and Improve Process Capability by:
- Utilizing Just-In-Time Principles to Eliminate All Non-Value-Added Processes and Activities
- Utilizing Statistical Process Control Analytical Techniques to Improve All Value-Added Processes
- Utilizing the CARE Process Improvement Team Roadmap

Develop Supplier Relationships That Continually Measure and Improve the Quality of Materials and Services Received

Continually Measure and Improve First-Run Yield:
- The Elimination of Any Defect in the Manufacturing Process Increases First-Run Yield
- As First-Run Yield Increases, Average Cycle Time per Unit Processed Decreases and Cost Per Unit Decreases

Continually Measure and Improve Equipment Effectiveness
- Increase Equipment Utilization
- Increase Equipment Uptime

SYSTEMS AND MEASUREMENTS

Systems and Measurements Will Focus on Those Value-Added Processes Important to Customer Satisfaction

"Real Time" Information Will Be a Priority in System Design to Reduce Cycle Time of All Processes

Performance Measurements Will Benchmark Against "Best-In-Class"

ENDNOTES

[1] Geraldine Fabrikant, "Debt Trips Up Hinckley, Venerable Yacht Maker," *New York Times*, October 9, 2009. https://www.nytimes.com/2009/10/10/business/10hinckley.html.

[2] Antione Drean, "10 Predictions for Private Equity in 2018," *Forbes Online*, January 24 2018. https://www.forbes.com/sites/antoinedrean/2018/01/24/ten-predictions-for-private-equity-in-2018/#c39fbf1319eb.

[3] Asa Bjornberg, Heinz-Peter Elstrodt, and Vivek Pandit, "The Family-Business Factor in Emerging Markets," *McKinsey Quarterly*, December 2014. https://www.mckinsey.com/featured-insights/winning-in-emerging-markets/the-family-business-factor-in-emerging-markets.

[4] Marnix van Rij et al., "How Is External Talent Accelerating the Growth of Family Businesses?" Family Business | EY Growth Barometer 2017. https://familybusiness.ey-vx.com/pdfs/ey-growth-barometer-family-business-report.pdf.

[5] Joseph H. Astrachan and Melissa Carey Shanker, "Family Business' Contribution to the U.S. Economy: A Closer Look," *Family Business Review* 16, no. 3 (2003):211-219. https://onlinelibrary.wiley.com/doi/abs/10.1111/j.1741-6248.2003.tb00015.x.

[6] Edelman Trust Barometer Survey, January 21, 2017. https://www.edelman.com/research/2017-edelman-trust-barometer.

[7] John T. O'Hara and Peter Mandel, "The World's Oldest Companies," *Family Business*, Spring 2002.

[8] Camille Egloff and Vikram Bhalla, "Governance for Family Businesses: Sustaining the 'Magic' for Generations to Come," *BCG Online*, October 20, 2014. https://www.bcg.com/publications/2014/corporate-strategy-portfolio-management-leadership-talent-governance-family-business.aspx.

[9] Mark J. Perry, "Fortune 500 Firms in 1955 vs. 2014; 88% Are Gone, and We're All Better Off Because of That Dynamic 'Creative Destruction'," American Enterprise Institute, August 18, 2014. http://www.aei.org/publication/fortune-500-firms-in-1955-vs-2014-89-are-gone-and-were-all-better-off-because-of-that-dynamic-creative-destruction/.

[10] Nadine Kammerlander and Marc van Essen, "Research: Family Firms Are More Innovative Than Other Companies," *Harvard Business Review*, January 25, 2017. https://hbr.org/2017/01/research-family-firms-are-more-innovative-than-other-companies.

[11] Carrie Hall and Marnix van Rij, "Is Adaptation or Disruption the Secret to Longevity?" EY, April 20, 2018. https://www.ey.com/en_gl/growth/is-adaptation-or-disruption-the-secret-to-longevity.

[12] Astrachan and Shanker, *Family Business Review*, 2003.

[13] Michael Hammer, "Deep Change: How Operational Innovation Can Transform Your Company," *Harvard Business Review,* April 2004, 84.

[14] Clayton M. Christensen, *The Innovator's Dilemma: The Revolutionary Book That Will Change the Way You Do Business* (New York: HarperBusiness, 2011).

[15] Nathan Bennett and Stephen A. Miles, *Riding Shotgun: The Role of the COO* (Redwood City, CA: Stanford Business Books, 2006).

[16] Nathan Bennett, "Second in Command: The Misunderstood Role of the Chief Operating Officer," *Harvard Business Review*, May 2006, 55.

[17] The Miles Group, "Riding Shotgun: The Role of the COO—Trailblazing Study of the Role of Chief Operating Officer—Updated and Released by Stanford Business Books," January 11, 2017. https://www.prnewswire.com/news-releases/riding-shotgun-the-role-of-the-coo---trailblazing-study-of-the-role-of-chief-operating-officer---updated-and-released-by-stanford-business-books-300389534.html.

[18] "Long-term Growth of Family Businesses Threatened by Accelerating Demographic Shifts, Disruption and Lack of Skilled Talent," EY Online, September 21, 2017. https://www.ey.com/gl/en/newsroom/news-releases/news-ey-long-term-growth-of-family-businesses-threatened-by-accelerating-demographic-shifts-disruption-and-lack-of-skilled-talent.

[19] Egloff and Bhalla, *BCG Online*, 2014.

[20] M. E. Porter, "How Competitive Forces Shape Strategy," *Harvard Business Review* 57, no. 2 (March–April 1979): 137–45.

[21] Marnix van Rij, "Why Family Businesses Are Growing Faster Than Their Peers," EY Online, July 5, 2018. https://www.ey.com/en_gl/growth/growth-barometer-family-business.

[22] Marnix van Rij, Carrie Hall, and Joe Astrachan, "Staying Power: How Do Family Businesses Create Lasting Success?" EY and Kennesaw State University, 2014. https://www.ey.com/Publication/vwLUAssets/ey-staying-power-how-do-family-businesses-create-lasting-success/$FILE/ey-staying-power-how-do-family-businesses-create-lasting-success.pdf.

[23] Egloff and Bhalla, *BCG Online*, 2014.

[24] Leon Danco and Donald Jonovic, *Outside Directors in the Family Owned Business* (Cleveland, OH: Center for Family Business, 1987).

[25] Craig Aronoff and John L. Ward, *Family Business Governance: Maximizing Family and Business Potential* (New York: Palgrave Macmillan, 2011).

[26] van Rij, et al., EY and Kennesaw State University, 2014.

[27] Edelman Family Trust Barometer Survey, 2017. https://www.edelman.com/research/2017-edelman-trust-barometer.

[28] Leslie Dashew, "Sustaining the Family Business," Aspen Family Business Institute. https://www.aspenfamilybusiness.com/pdf/eNews/Sustaining%20the%20Family%20Business%20by%20Leslie%20Dashew.pdf.

[29] John L. Ward, *Perpetuating the Family Business: 50 Lessons Learned from Long Lasting, Successful Families in Business* (London: Palgrave Macmillan UK, 2004).

[30] Family Business Alliance, "Cited Stats," 2018. https://www.fbagr.org/resources/cited-stats/.

RECOMMENDED READING

BOOKS IN BIBLIOGRAPHY

The Innovator's Dilemma: The Revolutionary Book That Will Change the Way You Do Business, Clayton M. Christensen

Riding Shotgun: The Role of the COO, Nathan Bennett and Stephen A. Miles

Outside Directors in the Family Business, Leon Danco and Donald Jonovic

Family Business Governance: Maximizing Family and Business Potential, Craig Aronoff and John L. Ward

Perpetuating the Family Business: 50 Lessons Learned from the Long Lasting Successful Families in Business, John L. Ward

ADDITIONAL RECOMMENDED READING

Inside the Family Business, Leon Danco

Leading Change, John P. Kotter

Hidden Champions: Lessons from 500 of the World's Best Unknown Companies, Hermann Simon

Built to Last, Jim Collins (James C. Collins?) and Jerry I. Porras

Five Forces, Michael Porter

Jack: Straight from the Gut, Jack Welch

China Inc., Ted C. Fishman

The Lexus and the Olive Tree, Thomas L. Friedman

Care of the Soul, Thomas Moore

ABOUT THE AUTHOR

Richard Seaman is the Chairman of Seaman Corporation, where he served as CEO from 1976 to 2015. He graduated in 1968 from Bowling Green State University with an MBA and joined the family business, which his father had founded in 1949. He assumed the leadership role of this family business in 1978 when his father passed away at the young age of fifty-five. Under his leadership, Seaman Corporation grew from $10 million in annual sales to nearly $200 million in sales today.

Richard serves as a Trustee of the Burton D. Morgan Foundation, a philanthropic organization dedicated to strengthening the free enterprise system by providing grants to organizations and institutions that foster the entrepreneurial spirit. In 2012 he was asked by the Governor of the State of Ohio to serve as a Commissioner of the State's Ohio Third Frontier, a multi-million-dollar economic initiative focused on the creation of a statewide technology-based entrepreneurial ecosystem.

Shortly after his father passed away, Richard joined the Young Presidents Organization and actively participated in their programs designed to create "Better Presidents through Education." He was an enthusiastic participant in the YPO Harvard Presidents' Program, which engages CEOs from around the world to discuss global economic issues and leading-edge business thinking. He continues his support for ongoing education by serving as a Trustee on the board of the College of Wooster.

Because of Richard's interest in multigenerational family business, he was asked to serve on the board of the Family Business Network–USA, where he has the opportunity to interact with multigenerational family businesses from around the world.

In 2012 Richard was recognized as an Honored Life Member of his industry trade organization, the Industrial Fabrics Association International, for his contribution to the industry. In 2014 he was recognized for

RECOMMENDED READING

BOOKS IN BIBLIOGRAPHY

The Innovator's Dilemma: The Revolutionary Book That Will Change the Way You Do Business, Clayton M. Christensen

Riding Shotgun: The Role of the COO, Nathan Bennett and Stephen A. Miles

Outside Directors in the Family Business, Leon Danco and Donald Jonovic

Family Business Governance: Maximizing Family and Business Potential, Craig Aronoff and John L. Ward

Perpetuating the Family Business: 50 Lessons Learned from the Long Lasting Successful Families in Business, John L. Ward

ADDITIONAL RECOMMENDED READING

Inside the Family Business, Leon Danco

Leading Change, John P. Kotter

Hidden Champions: Lessons from 500 of the World's Best Unknown Companies, Hermann Simon

Built to Last, Jim Collins (James C. Collins?) and Jerry I. Porras

Five Forces, Michael Porter

Jack: Straight from the Gut, Jack Welch

China Inc., Ted C. Fishman

The Lexus and the Olive Tree, Thomas L. Friedman

Care of the Soul, Thomas Moore

ABOUT THE AUTHOR

Richard Seaman is the Chairman of Seaman Corporation, where he served as CEO from 1976 to 2015. He graduated in 1968 from Bowling Green State University with an MBA and joined the family business, which his father had founded in 1949. He assumed the leadership role of this family business in 1978 when his father passed away at the young age of fifty-five. Under his leadership, Seaman Corporation grew from $10 million in annual sales to nearly $200 million in sales today.

Richard serves as a Trustee of the Burton D. Morgan Foundation, a philanthropic organization dedicated to strengthening the free enterprise system by providing grants to organizations and institutions that foster the entrepreneurial spirit. In 2012 he was asked by the Governor of the State of Ohio to serve as a Commissioner of the State's Ohio Third Frontier, a multi-million-dollar economic initiative focused on the creation of a statewide technology-based entrepreneurial ecosystem.

Shortly after his father passed away, Richard joined the Young Presidents Organization and actively participated in their programs designed to create "Better Presidents through Education." He was an enthusiastic participant in the YPO Harvard Presidents' Program, which engages CEOs from around the world to discuss global economic issues and leading-edge business thinking. He continues his support for ongoing education by serving as a Trustee on the board of the College of Wooster.

Because of Richard's interest in multigenerational family business, he was asked to serve on the board of the Family Business Network–USA, where he has the opportunity to interact with multigenerational family businesses from around the world.

In 2012 Richard was recognized as an Honored Life Member of his industry trade organization, the Industrial Fabrics Association International, for his contribution to the industry. In 2014 he was recognized for his long-term community leadership by being selected as a Wall of Fame Honoree by the Wooster Area Chamber of Commerce. In 2015 Richard was selected by Ernst & Young as Entrepreneur of the Year in the Family Business category.

Richard is an avid skier, sailor, photographer, and tennis player. Richard and his wife, Judy, live in Wooster, Ohio. They and the families of their three children are committed to being active owners and stewards of their family business enterprise.

www.vibrant-vision.com